CLASSROOM CONNECTIONS

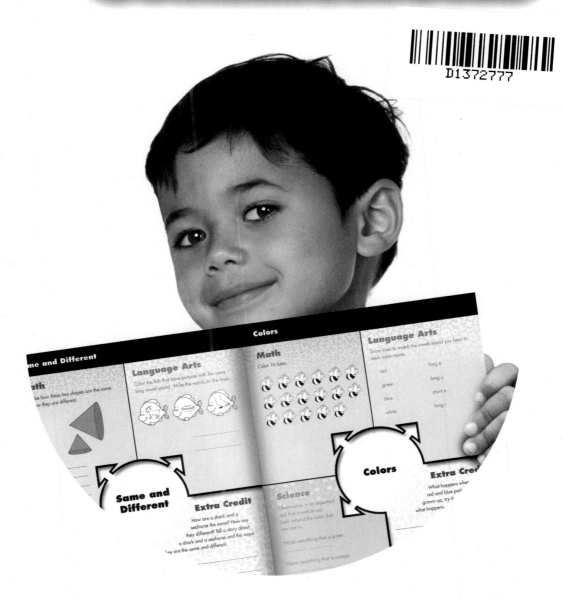

Thinking Kids™
An imprint of Carson-Dellosa Publishing LLC
Greensboro, North Carolina

Thinking Kids™
An imprint of Carson-Dellosa Publishing LLC
P.O. Box 35665
Greensboro, NC 27425 USA

Printed in the USA • All rights reserved.   ISBN 978-1-4838-1289-2
01-134157811

Welcome to *Classroom Connections!*

Classroom Connections is a unique series that shows your first grader how math, language arts, and science can all be tied together! Math isn't just math and language arts isn't just language arts – skills for these subjects can be connected across the learning spectrum, and with *Classroom Connections*, we'll show you how!

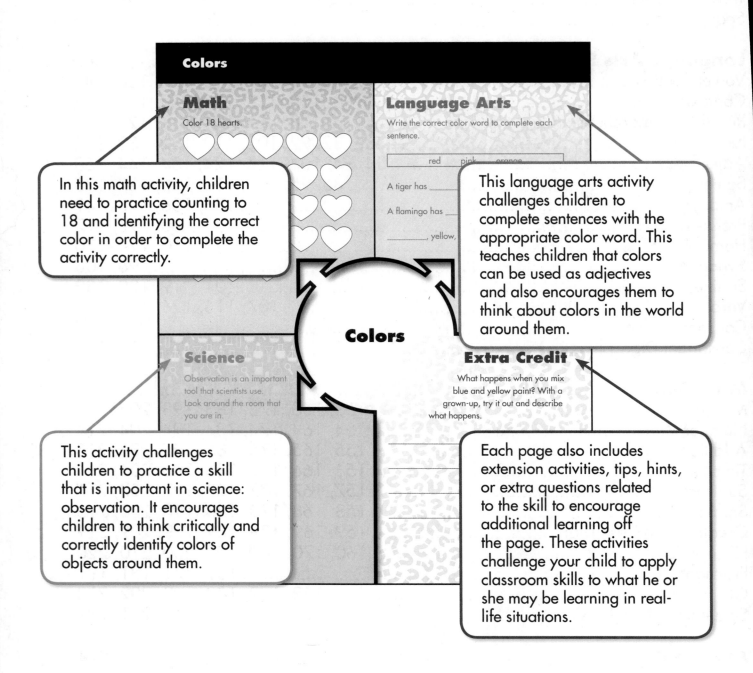

Colors

Math
Color 18 hearts.

Language Arts
Write the correct color word to complete each sentence.

red   pink   orange

A tiger has _____

A flamingo has _____

_____, yellow,

Colors

Science
Observation is an important tool that scientists use. Look around the room that you are in.

Extra Credit
What happens when you mix blue and yellow paint? With a grown-up, try it out and describe what happens.

In this math activity, children need to practice counting to 18 and identifying the correct color in order to complete the activity correctly.

This language arts activity challenges children to complete sentences with the appropriate color word. This teaches children that colors can be used as adjectives and also encourages them to think about colors in the world around them.

This activity challenges children to practice a skill that is important in science: observation. It encourages children to think critically and correctly identify colors of objects around them.

Each page also includes extension activities, tips, hints, or extra questions related to the skill to encourage additional learning off the page. These activities challenge your child to apply classroom skills to what he or she may be learning in real-life situations.

Classroom Connections is divided into three sections: Basic Skills, Language Arts, and Math. In the Basic Skills section, children will review the following topics and how they can be applied to Language Arts, Math, and Science:

- Classifying
- Matching
- Same and Different
- True and False
- Colors
- Critical Thinking
- Sequencing

For a brief review of these skills, turn to page 6.

In the Language Arts section, children will review the following topics and how they can be applied to Math and Science:

- Vowel Sounds
- Consonant Blends
- Consonant Digraphs
- Nouns
- Verbs
- Adjectives
- Sentences
- Synonyms
- Antonyms
- Prefixes
- Suffixes
- Homophones
- Context Clues
- Reading Comprehension

For a brief review of these skills, turn to page 77.

In the Math section, children will review the following topics and how they can be applied to Language Arts and Science:

- Shapes
- Number Words
- Addition
- Subtraction
- Time
- Greater Than/ Less Than
- Place Value
- Fractions
- Measurement
- Graphing
- Sequencing Numbers

For a brief review of these skills, turn to page 151.

Give your child the building blocks he or she needs for school success with the fun cross-curricular practice in this workbook. Grab a pencil, and get going!

Basic Skills Introduction

This Basic Skills section will address the following skills that first graders need to know:

Classifying
First graders will practice sorting, or classifying, objects into different categories that go together. Objects can be sorted by various categories, such as size, shape, and color.

Matching
First graders will practice identifying and drawing shapes and objects that match, such as two blue squares or three red kites.

Same and Different
First graders will learn to analyze and identify shapes and objects as being the same or different.

True and False
First graders will be asked to ask and answer questions about key details in a text. True/false questions typically give a statement that is either accurate or inaccurate, and children are asked to answer appropriately.

Colors
First graders will continue to work with and identify the colors red, yellow, blue, green, orange, purple, black, and brown.

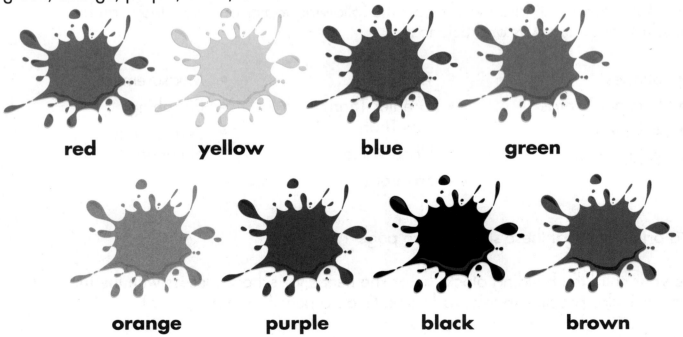

red   yellow   blue   green

orange   purple   black   brown

Critical Thinking

First graders will be asked to think critically and use logical reasoning to draw their own conclusions from stories they've read, rather than simply reading the author's conclusions that are clearly stated. This may include asking and answering questions about a text, comparing and contrasting events or characters, and using illustrations to describe a character, setting, or events.

Sequencing

Sequencing is putting a series of events in the correct order. First graders will work with sequencing in a variety of ways. They may be asked to put a series of pictures in the correct order, using critical thinking to determine what happens first, next, and last. Similarly, first graders may be asked to correctly sequence a series of numbers.

Math

Circle the things that are living.

How many things did you circle?

4

Language Arts

Name two ways these leaves could be sorted.

1. COLOR

2. _____

Classifying

Science

Tia sorted the animals into two groups. Fill in the top of the chart to show how she sorted them.

FLY	NO FLY
butterfly	cat
owl	worm
bee	snake
eagle	alligator

Extra Credit

Think of two ways you could sort your clothes.

FOLDING

1. _____

2. _____

Math

Draw lines to match.

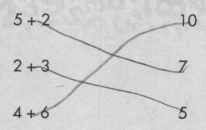

5 + 2   10

2 + 3   7

4 + 6   5

Language Arts

Draw lines to match.

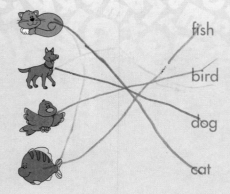

fish

bird

dog

cat

Matching

Science

Write the correct letter under each number to match each set of observations with where it would likely be found in a school.

1. classroom   A. Students are drinking
            milk. There are napkins
                and forks.

2. lunchroom   B. Students are holding
            pencils. There are desks.
                A teacher is writing on
                the board.

3. music room   C. Students are singing. The
                teacher is playing a
                song. There is a piano.

Extra Credit

Draw a set of matching mittens.

Math

Circle the problem that has a different sum.

3 + 5

4 + 4

2 + 4

2 + 6

1 + 7

Language Arts

Sort the words that have the same sounds.

| blow | my | carry | towel |
| why | ferry | flow | tower |

/ow/ as in **now**   towel   blown

/ō/ as in **snow**   blow   flow

/ī/ as in **fry**   why   my

/ē/ as in **berry**   ferry   carry

Same and Different

Science

Color the two animals that have the same kind of body covering.

Extra Credit

How are a bird and a cat the same? How are they different?

Animals

Math

Color 18 hearts.

Language Arts

Write the correct color word to complete each sentence.

red	pink	orange

A tiger has _____ and black stripes.

A flamingo has _____ feathers.

_____, yellow, and blue are primary colors.

Colors

Science

Observation is an important tool that scientists use. Look around the room that you are in.

Name something that is red.

_____

Name something that is blue.

_____

Name something that is yellow.

_____

Extra Credit

What happens when you mix blue and yellow paint? With a grown-up, try it out and describe what happens.

_____

_____

_____

_____

Math

Brad has 4 bananas and oranges in his bag. Draw pictures of all of the ways you can show the pieces of fruit in his bag.

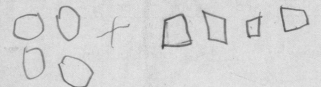

Language Arts

Look at the title below. The title can tell you what the story is about. What do you think the story will be about?

Art Class MAKEING PAINT

_____

_____

Critical Thinking

Science

Unscramble the words to complete the sentences.

You use your nose to _smell_ (lmsel).

You use your eyes to _see_ (ese).

You use your ears to _hear_ (erah).

You use your tongue to _taste_ (satet).

You use your hands to _touch_ (cuhto).

Extra Credit

Think of three words that begin with **b** and end with **d**.

1. _Bed_

2. _Bird_

3. _Bread_

Math

Write the word **true** or **false** on the line.

_____

$$1 + 9 = 9 + 1$$

Language Arts

Read each sentence. Circle **true** if it is a fact.
Circle **false** if it is not a fact.

1. Dogs have ears.

    (true) false

2. Rain is wet.

    (true) false

3. The beach does not have sand.

    true   (false)

True and False

Science

Read the sentences in the box. Then, read each sentence below. Circle whether the sentence is **true** or **false**.

All flowers are plants. Sunflowers are flowers.

Sunflowers are plants.

 (true) false

All plants are sunflowers.

 true (false)

Extra Credit

Name three things about your family that are true.

1. ___WE TVAL IT___
2. ___WE LIKE MONY___
3. ___WE LIKE ROOKS___

Math

Circle all of the even numbers.

30	2	13	17
23	12	8	25
1	7	10	14
11	16	41	4

Language Arts

Circle the pictures whose names have short vowel sounds.

Classifying

Science

Animals in the cat family have four legs, fur, and whiskers. They are meat eaters.

Write **C** next to each animal that is a cat. Write **N** next to each animal that is not a cat. Then, tell why it is not a cat.

1. _____ tiger
2. _____ eagle
3. _____ turtle

_____

_____

Extra Credit

Write a title for each group of items.

_____

fork   spoon   knife

_____

truck   car   boat

Math

Draw lines to match the problems and the sums.

2 + 6   5

3 + 6   6

4 + 3   7

1 + 4   8

3 + 3   9

Language Arts

Draw lines to match the words that have the same short vowel sounds.

sock   kit

camp   fog

mix   hand

Matching

Science

Draw a line to match each word with its definition.

float   when an object goes below the surface of a liquid

sink   when an object stays on top of a liquid

Extra Credit

Draw a set of matching boots.

Math

Circle the problem that has a different sum.

1 + 1

3 + 3

2 + 4

1 + 5

6 + 0

Language Arts

Color the fish that have pictures with the same long vowel sound. Write the words on the lines.

_____

_____

Same and Different

Science

Circle the items that are the same type of matter.

brick

water

smoke

juice

milk

Extra Credit

Take a walk around your home. Find two things that are the same, such as coats or shoes. In what ways are they the same? In what ways are they different?

_____

_____

_____

_____

Math

Color 20 stars.

Language Arts

Write the correct color word to complete each sentence.

blue	brown	green

The water on a globe is shown in_____.

Most plants and trees have _____ leaves in the spring.

A camel has _____ fur.

Colors

Science

Sort the objects in the word bank into two groups. Write a name for each group.

apple	orange	fire truck
carrot	strawberry	pumpkin

_____   _____

1. _____   1. _____

2. _____   2. _____

3. _____   3. _____

Extra Credit

What happens when you mix yellow and red paint? With a grown-up, try it out and describe what happens.

_____

_____

_____

_____

Math

Paul has 5 toy trucks and cars in a box. Draw a picture of all the ways you can show the vehicles in his box.

Language Arts

Some words have more than one meaning. Write another meaning for the word below.

1. **watch** – to look

2. **watch** – _____

Critical Thinking

Science

How might a scientist use math?

_____

_____

_____

Extra Credit

Think of three words that begin with **r** and end with **t**.

1. _____

2. _____

3. _____

Math

Write the number that makes the number sentence true.

10 + _____ = 15

6 + _____ = 10

1 + _____ = 5

0 + _____ = 0

Language Arts

Read each sentence. Circle **true** if it is a fact. Circle **false** if it is not a fact.

1. A bike has wheels.

   true   false

2. All cats have blue eyes.

   true   false

3. The word **ball** starts with the letter **r**.

   true   false

True and False

Science

Read the sentence in the box. Then, read each sentence below. Circle whether the sentence is **true** or **false**.

Insects are a kind of bug.

1. All bugs are insects.

   true   false

2. Insects are bugs.

   true   false

Extra Credit

Write three things about yourself that are false.

1. _____

2. _____

3. _____

Math

Circle all of the odd numbers.

18   2   29   17

3   4   8   26

23   12   7   51

13   19   22   44

Language Arts

Circle the pictures whose names have short vowel sounds.

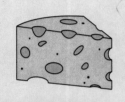
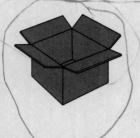

Classifying

Science

Circle the objects made of matter.

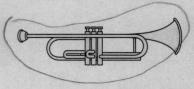

Extra Credit

Make a list of three things that are bumpy and three things that are smooth.

Bumpy
1. road
2. tree
3. glue

Smooth
1.
2.
3.

Math

Complete each number sentence.

If 7 + 2 = 9,
then 2 + 7 = ___.

If 3 + 5 = 8,
then 5 + 3 = ___.

If 1 + 6 = 7,
then 6 + 1 = ___.

Language Arts

Circle the picture that matches the adjective.

fast

Matching

Science

Draw lines to match the
science tool with its name.

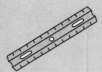

ruler

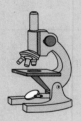

microscope

Extra Credit

Draw a set of matching ice
skates.

Math

Describe how these two shapes are the same and how they are different.

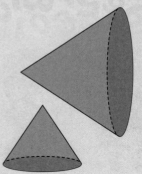

_____

_____

_____

_____

Language Arts

Color the fish that have pictures with the same long vowel sound. Write the words on the lines.

_____

_____

Same and Different

Science

Circle each word that means something is dangerous.

| recycle | hazard | poison |
| flammable | natural | |

Have you seen any of these words before? Describe where you saw it.

_____

_____

Extra Credit

How are a shark and a seahorse the same? How are they different? Tell a story about a shark and a seahorse and the ways they are the same and different.

_____

_____

_____

_____

Math

Color 16 bees.

Language Arts

Draw lines to match the vowel sound you hear in each color name.

red   long e

green   long u

blue   short e

white   long i

Colors

Science

Observation is an important tool that scientists use. Look around the room that you are in.

Name something that is green.

_____

Name something that is orange.

_____

Name something that is purple.

_____

Extra Credit

What happens when you mix red and blue paint? With a grown-up, try it out and describe what happens.

_____

_____

_____

_____

Math

Hector has 7 players on his baseball team. Some are boys and some are girls. Draw pictures of all the ways you can show the players on Hector's team.

Language Arts

Some words have more than one meaning. Write another meaning for the word below.

1. can – to be able to do something

2. can – _____

Critical Thinking

Science

Unscramble the words to complete the science safety rules.

1. Be sure to tie back long _____ (airh).

2. Never eat _____ (ofod) while doing science experiments.

3. Do not _____ (ridnk) liquids you are working with in science experiments.

Extra Credit

Name two science tools a scientist might use when observing a forest.

1. _____

2. _____

Math

Write the word **true** or **false** on the line.

_____

$4 + 5 = 5 + 4$

Write your own math equation that is true.

_____

Write your own math equation that is false.

_____

Language Arts

Read each sentence. Circle **true** if it is a fact. Circle **false** if it is not a fact.

1. Books do not have pages.

   true   **false**

2. Plants need sun to grow.

   true   **false**

3. Butterflies cannot fly.

   true   **false**

True and False

Science

Circle whether the following fact is **true** or **false**.

If you set two magnets near each other, they may pull towards one another.

   true   **false**

Extra Credit

Think of three true things about trees.

1. _____

2. _____

3. _____

Math

Circle all of the numbers that are greater than 10.

10	9	11	20
8	15	17	22
7	13	6	40
37	1	2	14

Language Arts

Circle the three pictures whose names have short vowel sounds.

Classifying

Science

Sort the objects in the word box into two groups.

ice	soup	milk	fire	snow

Extra Credit

Think of two different ways that you could sort a rock collection.

1. _____

2. _____

Math

Complete each number sentence.

If 4 + 6 = 10,
then 6 + 4 = _____.

If 8 + 7 = 15,
then 7 + 8 = _____.

If 3 + 9 = 12,
then 9 + 3 = _____.

Language Arts

Draw lines to match each adjective to the stronger adjective.

big   tiny

small   giant

hot   icy

cold   boiling

Matching

Science

Draw lines to match the science tool with its name.

goggles

hand lens

Extra Credit

Draw a set of matching skis.

Math

Describe how these two shapes are the same and how they are different.

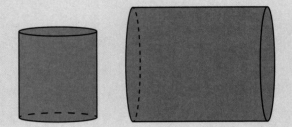

_____
_____
_____
_____

Language Arts

Circle the word pairs that have the same meaning.

1. friend   enemy

2. hard   difficult

3. tired   sleepy

4. happy   glad

5. unhappy   sad

Same and Different

Science

Name three different bodies of water.

1. _____

2. _____

3. _____

Extra Credit

What things are the same about a motorcycle and a bicycle? What things are different?

_____
_____
_____
_____

Math

Follow the directions. Write the number sentence.
Color 5 frogs blue. Color 3 frogs orange.

_____ + _____ = _____

Language Arts

Write two sentences. Use one color word from
the word box in each sentence.

purple	black

1. _____

_____

2. _____

_____

Colors

Science

Design a colorful bumper
sticker for a car with a
message about helping
our planet.

Extra Credit

Purple, orange, and green
are secondary colors. By
mixing two primary colors
together, you can make secondary
colors. Use purple, orange, and green to
draw a picture here.

Math

Write three facts about the number 15.

1. _____

2. _____

3. _____

Language Arts

Mario is writing a paragraph about ladybugs. Draw a line through any sentences that are opinions.

Ladybugs are insects. They are pretty. Ladybugs eat aphids. Aphids are bad. They eat crops. Ladybugs have two sets of wings. They lift their top wings and use their thinner wings beneath to fly. They fly fast.

Critical Thinking

Science

Write **F** is something is a fact and **O** if something is an opinion.

1. _____ Apples taste good.

2. _____ Apples are a fruit.

3. _____ Apples grow on trees.

4. _____ An apple tree is pretty.

Extra Credit

A fact is something that is proven to be true. An opinion is how a person feels about something.

1. Write a sentence that is a fact.

_____

_____

2. Write a sentence that is an opinion.

_____

_____

Math

Write the numbers that make the number sentences true.

8 + _____ = 13

3 + _____ = 10

_____ + 9 = 14

2 + _____ = 9

Language Arts

Read each sentence. Circle **true** if it is a fact. Circle **false** if it is not a fact.

1. Snow is warm.

   true   **false**

2. The word **cat** starts with the letter **c**.

   true   **false**

3. A ball has the shape of a cube.

   true   **false**

True and False

Science

Circle whether the following sentence is **true** or **false**.

If you set two magnets near each other, they may push away from one another.

true   **false**

Extra Credit

Write three things that are not true about your town.

1. _____

2. _____

3. _____

Math

Circle the shapes that have four sides.

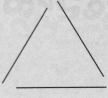

Language Arts

Color the three pictures whose names have short vowel sounds.

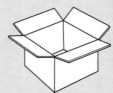

Classifying

Science

Energy causes things to move.

1. List six things that move.

_____ _____

_____ _____

_____ _____

2. Name a way you could sort the items.

_____

Extra Credit

Name two ways that you could sort a group of all kinds of dogs.

1. _____

2. _____

Math

Complete each number sentence.

If 8 + 7 = 15,
then 7 + 8 = _____.

If 1 + 2 = 3,
then 2 + 1 = _____.

If 9 + 8 = 17,
then 8 + 9 = _____.

Language Arts

Draw lines to match the words to make compound words.

grass	noon
school	board
skate	hopper
after	out
with	house

Matching

Science

Draw a line to match the safety equipment to its use.

1. fire extinguisher   A. to clean up spills

2. latex gloves   B. to put out fires

3. paper towels   C. to protect the hands

4. goggles   D. to protect the eyes

Extra Credit

Draw two bears wearing matching hats.

Math

Seth likes to watch movies. Last week, he watched 5 funny movies. Then, he watched 2 sports movies. Complete each sentence with the correct number.

Seth watched _____ funny movies.

Seth watched _____ sports movies.

Seth watched _____ movies in all.

Language Arts

Circle the words that have the same endings.

walked   walking   walks

talked   walker

Same and Different

Science

How are the sun and the moon the same?

_____

_____

How are they different?

_____

_____

Extra Credit

Name three ways that people differ from animals.

1. _____

2. _____

3. _____

Math

Use two different colors to show how you and a friend can equally share this candy bar.

Language Arts

Write two sentences. Use one color word from the word box in each sentence.

gray	orange

1. _____

   _____

2. _____

   _____

Colors

Science

Color the animals that can fly blue.

Extra Credit

How would you turn red paint into pink paint?

_____

_____

_____

Math

Greg has 2 different pieces of candy in his pocket. Draw a picture of all the ways you can show the different candy in Greg's pocket.

Language Arts

Some words have more than one meaning. Write another meaning for the word below.

1. **mouse** – computer part or tool

2. **mouse** – _____

Critical Thinking

Science

What will happen if you hold a strong magnet next to a metal paper clip? Circle the correct answer.

A. The paper clip will be pulled toward the magnet.

B. The paper clip will move away from the magnet.

C. Nothing will happen.

Extra Credit

Maria has just built a tall tower of blocks. Her 2-year-old brother is walking toward her. Predict what you think will happen next.

_____

_____

_____

_____

Math

Write the number that makes the number sentence true.

_____ + 7 = 15

_____ + 4 = 9

_____ + 6 = 13

Language Arts

Read each sentence. Circle **true** if it is a fact. Circle **false** if it is not a fact.

1. Ice is cold.

   true   **false**

2. The word **dog** starts with the letter **d**.

   true   **false**

3. A book has the shape of a cylinder.

   true   **false**

True and False

Science

Circle whether the following fact is **true** or **false**.

All metals are magnetic.

   true   **false**

Extra Credit

Write two things that are true about magnets.

1. _____

2. _____

Math

Write the sums. Circle the sums that are greater than 10.

1. 2 + 8 = _____

2. 3 + 9 = _____

3. 5 + 6 = _____

4. 8 + 1 = _____

Language Arts

Color the three pictures whose names have long vowel sounds.

Classifying

Science

Cats are part of the feline family. Circle three members of the feline family.

hen

cheetah ← Felines →

monkey

tiger

lion

ape

Extra Credit

What are two ways that the feline family members are alike?

1. _____

2. _____

Math

Complete the number sentence.

If $8 + 8 + 2 = 18$, then $8 + 2 + 8 = $ _____ .

Write your own number sentence like the one above. See if a friend can solve it.

_____

Language Arts

Draw lines to match the animals to the correct jobs.

dogs   catch mice

horses   herd sheep

cows   lay eggs

chickens   pull carts

cats   give milk

Matching

Science

Write the letter to match the object with its shape.

1. _____   2. _____

3. _____   4. _____

A. rectangular prism   B. cylinder

C. sphere   D. cone

Extra Credit

Draw a ladybug with dots that match on each side of its body.

Math

Complete each number sentence.

If 5 + 3 = 8,
then 3 + 5 = _____.

If 13 + 6 = 19,
then 6 + 13 = _____.

If 11 + 12 = 23,
then 12 + 11 = _____.

Language Arts

Circle the words below that have the same **/oo/** sound as in loop.

stone   spoon   spine

toot   moon

Same and Different

Science

What is the same about these two animals?

_____

_____

_____

Extra Credit

What is the same about a lion and a pet cat? What is different?

_____

_____

_____

Math

There are three red pencils. There are two blue pencils. How many pencils are there in all? Write the number sentence.

_____ + _____ = _____

Language Arts

Write two questions. Use one color word from the word box in each sentence.

pink	green

1. _____

   _____

2. _____

   _____

Colors

Science

Color the animals hidden in the habitat.

Extra Credit

How would you turn purple paint into lavender paint?

_____

_____

_____

_____

Math

Grace has 9 games on a shelf. Some of them are card games, and some of them are dice games. Draw a picture of all the ways you can show the games on Grace's shelf.

Language Arts

Some words have more than one meaning. Write another meaning for the word below.

1. **bark** – part of a tree

2. **bark** – _____

Critical Thinking

Science

Why do scientists wear safety goggles? Circle the correct answer.

A. to magnify what they are viewing

B. to protect their eyes

C. to make things look 3-D

Extra Credit

Describe three things that you do every day to stay safe.

1. _____

2. _____

3. _____

Math

Write <, >, or = to make the statement true.

27 〇 38

14 〇 13

7 〇 20

11 〇 11

Language Arts

Read the story. Circle the sentence that is true about the story.

My name is Myra, and I go to school. I go to school five days each week. Children go to school in many different places. I go to school in the city.

1. Myra goes to school in a small town.

2. Myra goes to school five days a week.

True and False

Science

Circle the sentence that is false.

1. A frog is a reptile.

2. A frog is an amphibian.

Extra Credit

Write two things that are true about penguins. Do some research with a grown-up if you need to.

1. _____

2. _____

Math

Write the sums. Circle the sums that are less than 10.

1. 3 + 8 = _____

2. 0 + 9 = _____

3. 7 + 6 = _____

4. 4 + 1 = _____

Language Arts

Color the three pictures whose names have long vowel sounds.

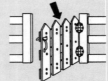

Classifying

Science

Dogs are part of the canine family. Circle three members of the canine family.

mouse

fox

coyote

Canines

ladybug

wolf

chicken

Extra Credit

What are two ways that the canine family members are alike?

1. _____

2. _____

Math

Complete the number sentence.

If $3 + 6 + 2 = 11$, then $6 + 2 + 3 =$ _____.

If $1 + 2 + 4 = 7$, then $4 + 1 + 2 =$ _____.

If $5 + 6 + 4 = 15$, then $6 + 4 + 5 =$ _____

Language Arts

Draw lines to match each uppercase letter to its lowercase letter.

Matching

Science

Match the word with the definition.

1. How someone feels about something   A. fact

2. Something that is true and can be proven   B. opinion

Extra Credit

Draw a pair of matching sneakers.

Math

If 9 + 8 + 1 = 18, then 8 + 1 + 9 = _____.

Write your own number sentence like the one above. See if a friend can solve it.

_____

Language Arts

Circle the words below that have the same **long o** sound, as in snow.

now   blow   crow

out   throw

Same and Different

Science

Describe what is different about the two pictures below.

_____

_____

Extra Credit

Name three different things that you do in gym class at school.

1. _____

2. _____

3. _____

Math

Use two different colors to show how you and a friend can equally share this pizza.

Language Arts

Write two exclamatory sentences. Use one color word from the word box in each sentence.

brown	yellow

1. _____

_____

2. _____

_____

Colors

Science

Color the ramp you think a toy car would move down the fastest.

Extra Credit

How could you make gray paint?

_____

_____

_____

_____

Math

Victor has 4 cats in his home. Some of the cats are white, and some of the cats are gray. Draw a picture of one of the ways you can show the cats in Victor's home.

Language Arts

Some words have more than one meaning. Write another meaning for the word below.

1. **ring** – jewelry on a finger

2. **ring** – _____

Critical Thinking

Science

Why is it a good idea to wash your hands after doing a science experiment?

_____

_____

_____

Extra Credit

Look out the window. What are some living things you see?

_____

_____

_____

Math

Write **true** or **false** on the line.

_____

$7 + 3 = 4 + 7$

Language Arts

Read the story and the sentences. Circle **true** or **false**.

My teacher is Ms. Moore. She likes to read and write. She also likes to do math. Ms. Moore tells our class to be kind and listen. She does not like it when the class gets too noisy!

1. Ms. Moore likes to read and write.

    true   **false**

3. Ms. Moore does not like to do math.

    true   **false**

True and False

Science

Circle if the following sentences are **true** or **false**.

1. The sun is cold.   true   false

2. The sun is a star.   true   false

3. The sun is smaller than Earth.   true   false

Extra Credit

Think of two things that are true about the sun.

1. _____

2. _____

Think of two things that are false about the sun.

1. _____

2. _____

Math

Write the differences. Circle the answers that are less than 10.

1. 12 – 3 = _____

2. 15 – 4 = _____

3. 10 – 6 = _____

4. 20 – 7 = _____

5. 10 – 2 = _____

Language Arts

Circle the words that are days of the week.

Sunday   December

August   Tuesday   Wednesday

Thanksgiving   Monday

Classifying

Science

Ostriches are part of the bird family. Circle three members of the bird family.

Extra Credit

What are two ways the bird family members are alike?

_____

_____

_____

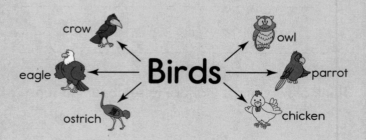

Math

Complete each number sentence.

If 11 + 6 = 17, then 6 + 11 = _____.

If 17 + 3 = 20, then 3 + 17 = _____.

If 5 + 19 = 24, then 19 + 5 = _____.

Language Arts

Circle the picture that matches the adjective.

cold

Matching

Science

Draw lines to match each object with the type of energy it uses.

bear   gasoline

bus   food

camp stove   fire

Extra Credit

Draw a hat and scarf that match.

Math

Write the answers to the problems. Circle the problems that have the same answer.

2 + 6 = _____

10 − 2 = _____

5 + 5 = _____

4 + 4 = _____

Language Arts

Circle the words below that have the same long i sound, as in pie.

lie   lit   flies

tie   tip

Same and Different

Science

Describe what is different about the two pictures below.

_____

_____

Extra Credit

What things are the same about a wolf and a dog? What things are different?

_____

_____

_____

_____

Math

Use two different colors to show how you and a friend can equally share this cookie.

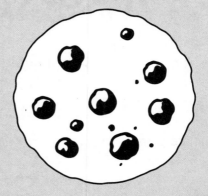

Language Arts

Circle the color word in each sentence.

1. I see a red truck.

2. My hamster has brown fur.

3. The clouds are puffy and white.

4. Dandelions are bright yellow.

Colors

Science

Color the things that are living.

Extra Credit

What two paint colors can you mix to make light blue?

_____

_____

Math

Cindy has 8 pets at home. Some of them are cats, and some of them are dogs. Draw a picture of all the ways you can show the pets at Cindy's house.

Language Arts

You can see a shadow when light is on one side of you. The light makes the shadow. When you are inside, lamps and flashlights make shadows. When you are outside, the sun makes shadows.

1. What makes shadows when you are inside?

    _____

2. Write a sentence about how a shadow is made.

    _____

    _____

    _____

Critical Thinking

Science

Complete the sentences. Unscramble the letters to fill in the missing words.

1. When ice melts, it changes to

    _____ (tewar).

2. When water freezes, it changes to

    _____ (cie).

3. When water boils, some of the water rises as water vapor, or _____ (eamst).

Extra Credit

Why do you think your shadow is tall sometimes and short other times?

_____

_____

_____

_____

Math

Write **true** or **false** on the line.

_____

$11 + 8 = 9 + 11$

Language Arts

Read the story and the sentences. Circle **true** or **false**.

Rice is a food. Many people in the world eat rice a few times a day. Almost all rice is grown in ponds. The rice crops need a lot of rain to grow.

1. Many people in the world eat rice.

    true   **false**

2. Rice crops do not need rain to grow.

    true   **false**

True and False

Science

Circle if the following sentences are **true** or **false**.

1. The sun is closer to Earth than the moon.   **true**   **false**

2. The sun is important to all living things on Earth.   **true**   **false**

Extra Credit

True or false?

George Washington was the first president of the United States.

_____

Math

Circle each problem that has an answer of 7.

5 + 2

8 – 1

6 – 4

6 + 2

9 – 5

Language Arts

Write the names of four things found in the trash.

Things in the Trash

Classifying

Science

Write **P** for plant and **A** for animal.

1. _____ tree

2. _____ dog

3. _____ ladybug

4. _____ leaf

5. _____ banana

6. _____ person

Extra Credit

Name two different ways that you could sort toy building blocks.

1. _____

2. _____

Math

Complete the number sentence.

If $8 + 3 = 11$, then $3 + 8 = $ _____.

Illustrate this number sentence using shapes.

Language Arts

Circle the picture that matches the adjective.

soft

Matching

Science

Draw lines to match each object with the type of energy it uses.

lamp   electricity

kite   sun

tree   wind

Extra Credit

Draw a picture of something that goes with this object.

Math

Number the objects as follows:

1 = long
2 = medium
3 = short

Language Arts

Write the words in ABC order on the train.

about   his   five

Sequencing

Science

Cara is doing an experiment to find whether objects sink or float. Read her steps below. Then, order the steps from **1-5**.

_____ Last, I cleaned up.

_____ Next, I collected my materials. I picked different objects to test.

_____ Then, I recorded my predictions.

_____ First, I cleaned off my work space.

_____ I put each object in the water and recorded what happened.

Extra Credit

List three things in order of how you get ready for school in the morning.

1. _____

2. _____

3. _____

Math

Complete each number sentence.

8 − 2 = 2 + _____

10 − 4 = 4 + _____

9 − 3 = 3 + _____

7 − 2 = 2 + _____

6 − 1 = 1 + _____

Language Arts

Circle the word pairs that have the same vowel sounds.

hoot   blew

fight   risk

boat   wrote

Same and Different

Science

Write **A** if the fact tells how sunflowers and apple trees are alike. Write **D** if the fact tells how they are different.

1. _____ has leaves

2 _____ has roots

3. _____ has bark

4. _____ makes seeds

5. _____ has branches

Extra Credit

How are a frog and a butterfly alike? How are they different?

_____

_____

_____

_____

Math

Jacob has 6 race cars. Some of them are red, and some of them are blue. Draw a picture of all the ways you can show Jacob's race cars.

Language Arts

Liv wanted to do one thing. She wanted to ride a horse. She loved horses. She read horse books at the library. She drew horses in art class. She had horse pictures in her room.

How do you know Liv loves horses? Write a sentence to explain.

_____

_____

Critical Thinking

Science

1. If you were to push the ball, what would happen?

_____

_____

2. Why? _____

_____

Extra Credit

What are three things that you notice when summer turns to fall?

1. _____

2. _____

3. _____

Math

Write the number that makes the number sentence true.

_____ + 5 = 7

_____ + 4 = 8

_____ + 2 = 9

_____ + 8 = 11

Language Arts

Read the story and the sentences. Circle **true** or **false**.

Sharks live in the ocean. They have been there for thousands of years. In the ocean, there are more than 350 kinds of sharks. Some sharks have big teeth. Others have small teeth.

1. All sharks have small teeth.

    true   **false**

2. There are more than 350 kinds of sharks.

    true   **false**

True and False

Science

Circle **true** or **false**.

Binoculars would help a scientist observe a bird high in a tree.

    true   **false**

Extra Credit

A dog is in the feline family of animals.

True or false?

_____

Math

Circle the numbers that are greater than 10, but less than 20.

11   8   22   19

17   6   14   76

21   9   32   13

7   18   66   41

Language Arts

Write the **hard c** words on the rock. Write the **soft c** words on the pillow.

cap   catch   cell   center   cup

Classifying

Science

Write **L** if the object is living. Write **N** if the object is nonliving.

1. _____ rock
2. _____ apple tree
3. _____ bird
4. _____ fish
5. _____ bike
6. _____ person

Extra Credit

What are two different ways that you could sort your books?

1. _____

2. _____

Math

Complete the number sentence.

If 10 + 2 = 12, then 2 + 10 = _____.

Illustrate this number sentence using shapes.

Language Arts

Circle the picture that matches the adjective.

hot

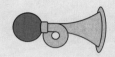 

Matching

Science

Match each word with its definition.

attract   1. magnetized tool that points north to help find direction

compass   2. to pull an object towards something

Extra Credit

Draw an item that goes with the item below.

Math

Number the objects as follows:

1 = long
2 = medium
3 = short

Language Arts

Write the words in ABC order on the train.

by   again   any

Sequencing

Science

Number the pictures in the order that an egg would become a butterfly.

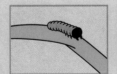
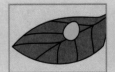

Extra Credit

List three things in order of how you get ready for bed at night.

1. _____

2. _____

3. _____

Math

Complete each number sentence.

$9 - 6 = 2 +$ _____

$12 - 3 = 3 +$ _____

$15 - 7 = 7 +$ _____

$13 - 5 = 5 +$ _____

$11 - 4 = 4 +$ _____

Language Arts

Circle the words that have the same ending sound

walk   talk   bench

wash   dock

Same and Different

Science

Circle the names of the animals that have the same body coverings.

shark   toad   robin

bear   owl   turkey

Extra Credit

What is the same about an owl and a penguin? What is different?

_____

_____

_____

_____

Math

Hannah has 5 leaves. Some of them are orange, and some of them are yellow. Draw a picture of all the ways you can show Hannah's leaves.

Language Arts

Ming went to see a play with her grandmother. Ming saw actors on the stage. They looked like they were having fun. When Ming went onstage at school, she felt bad. She felt dizzy. She wanted to have fun like the actors.

How do you know Ming is afraid of being onstage? Write a sentence to explain.

_____

_____

_____

Critical Thinking

Science

Circle **true** or **false**.

A scientist uses a microscope to see large objects smaller.

true   **false**

Extra Credit

A factual story is a true story. Write a factual story and draw a picture to go with it.

_____

_____

_____

_____

Math

Write the word **true** or **false** on the line.

_____

$7 + 8 = 8 + 7$

Language Arts

Read the story and the sentences. Circle **true** or **false**.

Maple syrup is sold in bottles at grocery stores. It tastes sweet. It is very sticky. It comes from trees. Maple trees have sap that comes out of them. First, the trees need to have holes drilled in them. Then, the sap drips out of the holes.

1. Maple syrup tastes salty.

   true   false

2. Sap comes from maple trees.

   true   false

True and False

Science

Circle **true** or **false**.

Binoculars would help a scientist observe a tiny insect.

   true   false

Extra Credit

A cat is in the canine family of animals.

True or false?

_____

Math

Circle all of the even numbers.

11	10	9	29
14	7	15	17
3	22	16	27
4	13	15	35

Language Arts

Write the **hard g** words on the rock. Write the **soft g** words on the pillow.

germ	get	giraffe	Gus	gust

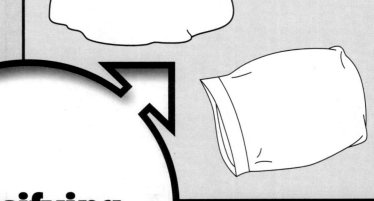

Classifying

Science

What makes something living? Discuss your answer with a friend.

_____

_____

_____

_____

_____

Extra Credit

Think of two ways that you could sort your favorite collection.

1. _____

2. _____

Math

Number the objects as follows:

1 = long
2 = medium
3 = short

_____   _____   _____

Language Arts

Write the missing days of the week in the correct order.

| Saturday | Monday | Wednesday |

Sunday, _____, Tuesday, _____,

Thursday, Friday, _____

Sequencing

Science

Put the following bodies of water in order from smallest to largest.

| lake | ocean | pond | puddle |

_____

_____

_____

_____

Extra Credit

Write a story about a time that you were proud. Make sure the story has a beginning, a middle, and an end.

_____

_____

_____

_____

Math

Complete each number sentence.

$7 - 4 = 2 + \underline{\quad}$

$12 - 8 = 1 + \underline{\quad}$

$16 - 4 = 4 + \underline{\quad}$

$11 - 1 = 3 + \underline{\quad}$

$15 - 2 = 2 + \underline{\quad}$

Language Arts

A prefix is a part of a word. It is at the beginning.

Draw a line to match each prefix to the correct meaning.

dis-	before
un-	not
re-	not
pre-	again

Matching

Science

Match each word with its definition.

magnet   1. an object that attracts materials made of iron or steel

repel   2. to push an object away from something

Extra Credit

Draw an item that goes with the item below.

Math

Kennedy collects bugs. She collected 13 ladybugs in one jar. She collected 5 lightning bugs in another jar. Complete each sentence with the correct number.

Kennedy collected _____ ladybugs.

Kennedy collected _____ lightning bugs.

Kennedy collected _____ bugs in all.

Language Arts

Circle the word pairs that sound the same.

one   won

big   bag

two   too

Same and Different

Science

Name three different things that plants need to grow.

1. _____

2. _____

3. _____

Extra Credit

What is the same about a shark and a goldfish? What is different?

_____

_____

_____

_____

Math

Number the items as follows:

1 = long
2 = medium
3 = short

___

___

___

Language Arts

Write the bug names in ABC order.

| grasshopper | ant | ladybug |
| caterpillar | centipede | |

1. _____

2 _____

3. _____

4. _____

5. _____

Sequencing

Science

Use the word bank to label the pictures of the life cycle of a pumpkin.

| flower | orange pumpkin | seed | vine |

___   sprout   ___

___   green pumpkin   ___

Extra Credit

Retell the story of Cinderella to a friend. What happens first? What happens next? What happens at the end?

_____

_____

_____

_____

Math

Sarah has 7 toy horses. Some of them are brown, and some of them are gray. Draw a picture of all the ways you can show Sarah's horses.

Language Arts

Josie is getting ready for bed. She is tired. She puts on her pajamas. Her cat Paws is under the bed. He hops out and jumps on Josie's pant leg. Josie screams! Paws surprises her. Then, Josie sees Paws run out of her room.

Why do you think Paws ran? Write a sentence.

_____

_____

Critical Thinking

Science

Circle the best answer.

Which would be better to use to collect water?

beaker   net   goggles

Extra Credit

What science tool would you use to look closely at a flower petal?

_____

Math

Write the word **true** or **false** on the line.

_____

$9 - 7 = 8 - 6$

Language Arts

Read the story. Circle **true** or **false**.

People read about global warming. It is in newspapers and books. People do not want Earth to be too warm. The weather changes. The animals move. Some deer moved north to where it is cooler.

1. People want Earth to be very warm.

    true   **false**

2. Global warming makes the weather change.

    true   **false**

True and False

Science

Circle true or false.

A scientist uses a hand lens to see small objects larger.

true   **false**

Extra Credit

Write three things that you know are true about butterflies.

1. _____

2. _____

3. _____

Math

Circle all the problems that have an answer of 7.

2 + 5

8 – 2

9 – 2

3 + 6

6 + 1

Language Arts

Write the names of different kinds of storms.

Kinds of Storms

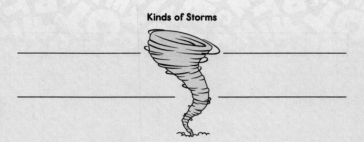

_____ _____

_____ _____

Classifying

Science

Put the following objects from smallest to largest.

| mouse | polar bear | human | cat |

_____

_____

_____

_____

Extra Credit

Think of two different ways that you can sort crayons.

1. _____

2. _____

Math

Write the numbers in order from smallest to largest.

| 10 | 4 | 7 | 9 | 1 | 3 |

_____

_____

_____

_____

_____

_____

Language Arts

Describe the steps to make a sandwich.

1. _____

_____

2. _____

_____

3. _____

_____

4. _____

_____

_____

Sequencing

Science

Write the numbers **1** to **5** to put the life cycle of a frog in order.

_____ A frog lays eggs in the water.

_____ Their front legs grow, and their tails get shorter. The gills are now covered. Their lungs being used. They are now adult frogs.

_____ A female adult frog lays eggs. The cycle starts over.

_____ Next, the tadpoles start to grow back legs. Their lungs grow.

_____ Then, the eggs hatch. The tadpoles each have a tail and gills.

Extra Credit

Draw a comic strip that shows the steps to make your favorite snack.

This Language Arts section will address the following skills that first graders need to know:

Vowel Sounds

Vowels are the letters **a**, **e**, **i**, **o**, and **u**. These letters can make both short and long vowel sounds. **Short a** makes the sound of **a** in **cat**. **Short e** makes the sound of **e** in **hen**. **Short i** makes the sound of **i** in **mitt**. **Short o** makes the sound of **o** in **box**. **Short u** makes the sound of **u** in **cup**. Long vowel sounds say their own name. For example, **long a** makes the sound of **a** in **cake**. **Long e** makes the sound of **e** in **seed**. **Long i** makes the sound of **i** in **kite**. **Long o** makes the sound of **o** in **rope**. **Long u** makes the sound of **u** in **cube**.

Consonant Blends

A consonant blend is when two consonants appear together. A blend can be at the beginning or the end of a word. Examples of words with blends are **gr**een, **sn**ake, and wa**nt**.

Consonant Digraphs

A consonant digraph is two letters that make a new sound. Examples of digraphs are **sh**out, **ch**ange, **wh**ale, and **th**ink.

Nouns

A noun is a person, place, thing, or idea. Examples of nouns are **girl**, **beach**, **car**, and **hope**. Proper nouns name a specific person, place, or thing, and should always begin with a capital letter. Examples of proper nouns are **Aunt Erma**, **Jefferson Elementary School**, and **Atlantic Ocean**.

Verbs

Verbs are action words. They are words that tell what a person or a thing can do. Examples of verbs are **eat**, **talk**, **jump**, **blink**, and **laugh**. Verbs can be in the past, present, or future tense. Examples of verbs in different tenses are **play** (present), **played** (past), and **will play** (future).

Adjectives

Adjectives are describing words. They give you more details about a noun. Examples of adjectives are the **furry** dog, the **tall** mountain, and the **green** leaf.

Sentences

Sentences should always begin with a capital letter and end with a punctuation mark. A statement is a sentence that tells something. It ends with a period. A question is a sentence that asks something. It ends with a question mark. An exclamatory sentence shows a lot of emotion. It ends with an exclamation point.

Synonyms

Synonyms are words that mean the same or almost the same thing. Examples of synonyms are **near** and **close**, **big** and **large**, and **run** and **jog**.

Antonyms

Antonyms are words that mean the opposite. Examples of antonyms are **strong** and **weak**, **tall** and **short**, and **soft** and **hard**.

Prefixes

A prefix is a word part. It is at the beginning of a word. Examples of prefixes are **pre**heat, **dis**cover, **re**cycle, and **un**do.

Suffixes

A suffix is a word part. It is at the end of a word. Examples of suffixes are happi**ly**, taste**ful**, bottom**less**, and teach**er**.

Homophones

Homophones are words that sound the same but are spelled differently. Examples of homophones are **aunt** and **ant**, **bear** and **bare**, and **blue** and **blew**.

Context Clues

Context clues are hints that an author gives to help the reader define an unfamiliar word or situation.

Reading Comprehension

Comprehension means that you understand what you are reading. First graders will be expected to ask and answer questions about both the main point and key details in books and texts that they have read to demonstrate clear understanding.

Math

Say the number words. Circle the number word that has the **long i** sound.

one

three

five

Language Arts

Color the picture whose name has the **long i** sound.

Vowel Sounds

Science

Sort the objects in the word bank into two groups. Then, circle the objects whose names have the **long i** sound.

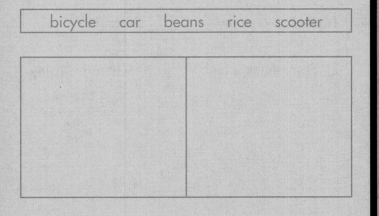

bicycle	car	beans	rice	scooter

Extra Credit

Can you think of a color name that has the **long i** sound?

_____

Math

Jan had 4 dolls. Two were lost. How many dolls does Jan have left?

_____ – _____ = _____

Jan has _____ dolls left.

Language Arts

Use a word from the box to complete each sentence.

stinky	tall	furry	blue	hot

1. The sky is _____.

2. The cat is _____.

3. The tree is _____.

4. The sock is

   _____.

5. The food is

   _____.

Context Clues

Science

Fill in the blank with one of the states of matter: **solid**, **liquid**, or **gas**.

1. Water is a _____. It takes the shape of its container.

2. A wooden block is a _____. It does not take the shape of its container.

3. Oxygen is a _____. It fills the space it is given.

Extra Credit

Circle the word that could complete both sentences.

blue	blew

1. Jill has a pretty _____ shirt.

2. Sometimes, I feel _____ when it is rainy.

Math

Dante has 9 apples. He gives away 3 apples. How many apples does Dante have left?

_____ – _____ = _____

Language Arts

Shadow play is fun. You can move your hands to show pictures. You can even show animals. Some animals you can make are farm animals such as ducks. You can make alligators and rabbits too.

1. What kind of shadows can you make with your hands?

   _____

2.. Name three animals you can make.

   _____

   _____

   _____

Reading Comprehension

Science

Read through Katie's journal entry to answer the questions.

Today, it was sunny out. I quickly put on my swimsuit and went outside. And there, on the sand, was a sea star! Then, I saw two pretty shells. When I went to pick one up, the water washed it away before I could grab it.

1. Where do you think Katie is?

   _____

2. What are some clues?

   _____

Extra Credit

If you have trouble with reading comprehension questions, what should you do?

_____

_____

_____

Math

Write three nouns that are people.

1. _____

2. _____

3. _____

Language Arts

Write a sentence using each noun from the word box.

horn	car	pumpkin

_____

_____

_____

Nouns

Science

The ranger helps care for the forest habitat. The forest is home to many plants and animals.

1. Write a noun from the sentences that is a person. _____

2. Write a noun from the sentences that is a place. _____

3. Write a noun from the sentences that is a thing. _____

Extra Credit

Remember: a noun is a person, place, thing, or idea. Write one of each kind of noun.

Person: _____

Place: _____

Thing: _____

Idea: _____

Math

Pam had 10 apples. Jan gave her 9 more. How many apples did Pam have in all?

_____

Write the **short a** words you find in the story problem above.

_____ _____ _____

_____ _____ _____

Language Arts

Circle the picture whose name has a **short a** sound.

Vowel Sounds

Science

Write a fact about bananas.

_____

_____

Write an opinion about bananas.

_____

How many times do you hear the **short a** vowel sound in the word bananas?

_____

Extra Credit

Write three words that have the **short a** sound.

_____

_____

_____

Adjectives

Math

Write the number word that describes each group.

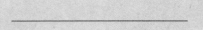 _____

  _____

_____

Language Arts

Write a sentence to describe a butterfly. Use two adjectives in your sentence.

_____

_____

Adjectives

Science

Use two words to describe each of the items found on Earth's surface.

1. sand _____, _____

2. mountain _____, _____

3. water _____, _____

Extra Credit

Remember, adjectives are words that describe nouns. Write your own sentence using at least two adjectives.

_____

_____

_____

Math

Write the correct answer to each number sentence.

3 + 3 = _____

4 + 1 = _____

2 + 2 = _____

3 + 7 = _____

Language Arts

Put a period at the end of each sentence.

1. The dog and the cat have fur

2. The fish like to swim

Sentences

Science

Write a sentence that tells what a scientist might use a camera for.

_____

_____

Extra Credit

A statement is a sentence that tells something. It ends with a period. Write a statement about what you are wearing today.

_____

_____

_____

Math

Write the word **true** or **false** on the line.

_____

$5 + 2 = 2 + 5$

Language Arts

Write one antonym for each word.

1. bottom _____

2. good _____

3. fast _____

4. up _____

Antonyms

Science

Write the opposite of each property of matter.

1. long _____

2. hot _____

3. heavy _____

4. bumpy _____

Extra Credit

Antonyms are words that have opposite meanings. How many antonym pairs can you think of?

_____

_____

_____

_____

Math

Prefix + Word = Meaning

Write the meaning of each new word.

1. dis + agree = _____

2. un + certain = _____

3. re + name = _____

Language Arts

Dis- means **not**. Write what each word means. The first one has been done for you.

1. disrespect   not respect

2. dishonest   _____

3. disobey   _____

4. dislike   _____

Prefixes

Science

Non- is a prefix that means **not**.

Sort the following things found on Earth into the chart.

water	trees	rocks	birds
minerals	grass	soil	

Living	Nonliving

Extra Credit

A prefix is a word part. It is at the beginning of a word. Write a word using each prefix below.

Pre- means **before**. _____

Dis- means **not**. _____

Re- means **again**. _____

Un- means **not**. _____

Math

Write a sentence with each homophone. Circle the homophone that is a number word.

1. ate _____

2. eight _____

Language Arts

Draw lines to match the homophones.

blew   blue

see   beat

beet   sea

Homophones

Science

Write the homophone for each word that is an insect name.

1. flee _____

2. aunt _____

3. be _____

Extra Credit

Homophones are words that sound the same but are spelled differently. Write three pairs of homophones.

1. _____ _____

2. _____ _____

3. _____ _____

Math

Say the number words. Circle the number word that has the **long a** sound.

two

four

eight

Language Arts

Color the picture whose name has the **long a** sound.

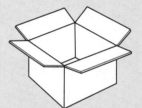

Vowel Sounds

Science

Fill in the blanks with words from the word bank. Circle the word that has the **long a** sound.

rays	skin	sun	sunblock

1. When you go out in the _____, it is

   important to protect your _____.

2. The sun's _____ can cause sunburns.

3. Wear _____ to prevent your skin
   from burning.

Extra Credit

Often, words with long vowels have the vowel-consonant-vowel pattern. Read the words below. Then, write three more **long a** words that have the vowel-consonant-vowel pattern.

cake	gate	tape

1. _____

2. _____

3. _____

Math

Nassim wrote 10 emails on Monday. He wrote 6 more emails on Tuesday. How many total emails did Nassim write on Monday and Tuesday?

Nassim wrote _____ total emails on Monday and Tuesday.

Language Arts

Complete the sentences. Unscramble the letters to fill in the missing words.

1. Plants may be used for shelters. Birds can make _____ (esnts) with plants.

2. Insects sometimes use plants to blend in. Green grasshoppers can _____ (idhe) in grass.

3. Many animals use plants as a food source. Pandas _____ (eta) bamboo.

Context Clues

Science

Fill in the blanks with words from the word bank.

insects	leaves	plants	soil

1. Worms break down dead leaves into _____.

2. Seeds that are replanted become new _____.

3. Animals plant parts like fruits and _____.

4. _____ help to pollinate flowers.

Extra Credit

Circle the word that could complete both sentences.

one	won

1. May I have _____ more cookie?

2. _____ of my friends has a skateboard.

Math

A biologist observed the plants and animals in and around a nearby pond. She counted what she saw.

lily pads: 4   frogs: 3   cattails: 4
birds: 6   wildflowers: 9   dragonflies: 2
turtles: 5

1. How many total plants did she find?
   _____ plants

2. How many total animals did she find? _____ animals

Language Arts

Myra's class has 15 children. Nine are girls, and six are boys. The class has a pet in a tank. He is a turtle. His name is Oscar. He eats lettuce and sits on a rock.

1. How many children are in Myra's classroom? _____

2. Where is the class pet? _____

3. What is the class pet's name? _____

Reading Comprehension

Science

A low-flow toilet uses about 6 liters of water each time it is flushed. A toilet that is not low-flow may use about 13 liters each time it is flushed.

1. How many liters of water will each type of toilet use if flushed 2 times in a day?
   low-flow: _____ liters
   not low-flow: _____ liters

2. How many liters of water would be saved each day with the low-flow toilet?
   _____ liters

Extra Credit

What does the word **comprehension** mean?

_____

_____

_____

Math

Write three nouns that are places.

1. _____

2. _____

3. _____

Language Arts

Rewrite each word beginning with a capital letter.

1. march _____

2. february _____

3. thursday _____

4. saturday _____

Nouns

Science

Circle the noun that best completes the sentence.

Animals use energy from _____ to live and to grow.

A. the sun

B. animals

C. plants

D. animals and plants

Extra Credit

A proper noun begins with a capital letter. The months of the year and days of the week are proper nouns. Write each month of the year.

_____

_____

_____

_____

Math

Write three words that rhyme with **sun**.

1. _____

2. _____

3. _____

What short vowel sound do you hear in all the words?

_____

Language Arts

Circle the picture whose name has the **short u** sound.

Vowel Sounds

Science

Fill in the missing vowels.

1. A r___l___r is used to measure the length of an object.

2. A m___cr___sc___pe helps scientists to see small objects larger.

Extra Credit

Write a sentence using the words **up**, **cup**, and **pup**.

_____

_____

_____

Math

Write the number word that describes each group.

  _____

  _____

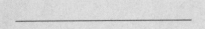

_____

Language Arts

Write two words to describe a caterpillar.

1. _____

2. _____

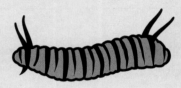

Adjectives

Science

Use two words to describe each of the items found on Earth's surface.

1. soil _____, _____

2. rock _____, _____

3. grass _____, _____

Extra Credit

What adjectives describe how you would feel on a cold, snowy day?

_____

_____

Math

Write the correct answer to each number sentence.

10 − 5 = _____

4 − 3 = _____

6 − 3 = _____

9 − 7 = _____

Language Arts

Put a period at the end of each sentence that tells something.

1. The mop is wet

2. The boy jumps up

3. Where are we going

Sentences

Science

Write a sentence that tells how a scientist could use her senses to observe the woods.

_____

_____

_____

Extra Credit

Sentences are everywhere! Look around your house to find sentences. You might find them on food packages, game instructions, your homework, and more! Write one of the sentences you found.

_____

_____

_____

Math

Write the correct answer to each question.

5 + 3 is the same as

3 + _____.

4 + 2 is the same as

2 + _____.

Language Arts

Write a synonym for each word.

1. kids _____

2. ladies _____

3. noisy _____

Synonyms

Science

Draw lines to match the weather words that are synonyms.

windy   wet

cold   breezy

rainy   chilly

Extra Credit

Synonyms are words that have the same meaning. Write three pairs of synonyms.

1. _____ _____

2. _____ _____

3. _____ _____

Math

Prefix + Word = Meaning

Write the meaning of each new word.

1. re + play = _____

2. pre + school = _____

3. un + happy = _____

Language Arts

Pre- means **before**. Write what each word means. The first one has been done for you.

1. pretest   test before

2. preteach   _____

3. precook   _____

4. preheat   _____

Prefixes

Science

Circle the prefix in each of the words below.

refuse

reduce

reuse

recycle

Extra Credit

Name three words that have the prefix re-, which means **again**.

1. _____

2. _____

3. _____

Math

Write a sentence with each homophone. Circle the homophone that is a number word.

1. two _____

_____

2. to _____

_____

Language Arts

Underlines the homophone pairs in each sentence.

1. Did you see the sea otter?

2. I would not want to be stung by a bee.

3. Do you know when this library book is due?

Homophones

Science

Fill in the blanks with the correct words.

hour	our

It took about an _____ to finish _____ experiment with frogs.

Extra Credit

Write a funny sentence using the homophones **chili** and **chilly**.

_____

_____

_____

Math

Say the number words. Circle the number word that has the **long e** sound.

one

three

ten

Language Arts

Color the picture whose name has the **long e** sound.

Vowel Sounds

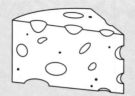

Science

Label the parts of the flower with words from the word bank. Circle the part that has the **long e** sound.

leaf	petal	root	stem

Extra Credit

Think of three words that rhyme with **cheese**. Then, write a poem using the rhyming words.

1. _____

2. _____

3. _____

_____

_____

Math

Maggie picks 6 flowers. Her mom gives her 2 more flowers. How many flowers does Maggie have?

Maggie has _____ flowers.

Language Arts

Read the story and answer the questions.

Lila's school is on a busy street in the city. A fence is around the outside of the school. There is a basketball hoop and court. There is also a playground with a slide.

1. Where is Lila's school?

   _____

2. List three things at Lila's school.

   _____

   _____

   _____

Reading Comprehension

Science

Olivia and Mason each built a bridge with toothpicks. They then tested which bridge was stronger by placing coins on top. Olivia's bridge held 29 pennies before it began to break. Mason's bridge held 24 nickels before it began to break.

1. What makes it hard to tell whose bridge was stronger?

   _____

   _____

Extra Credit

Tell what happens in your favorite part of your favorite book.

_____

_____

_____

_____

Math

Add the suffix -er to each word. Then, write the word.

1. call + er = _____

2. farm + er = _____

3. dream + er = _____

4. sing + er = _____

Language Arts

Write what each word means. The first one has been done for you.

1. painter   one who paints

2. seller   _____

3. bowler   _____

4. driver   _____

Suffixes

Science

Find and circle the suffix -er in each sentence below.

The speaker talked about how to grow vegetables.

She is an expert gardener.

Every listener was fascinated by her stories.

Extra Credit

A suffix is a word part. It is at the end of a word. Write a word using each suffix below.

-er means **one who** _____

-ful means **full of** _____

-less means **without** _____

-ly means **in a certain way** _____

Math

Write three nouns that are things.

1. _____

2. _____

3. _____

Language Arts

A noun is a person, place, thing, or idea. Write one noun to fit each of these categories.

1. person: _____

2. place: _____

3. thing: _____

4. idea: _____

Nouns

Science

Circle the noun that best completes the sentence.

Plants use energy from _____ to live and to grow.

A. animals
B. the sun
C. wind
D. other plants

Extra Credit

Examples of nouns that are ideas are **freedom**, **happiness**, and **friendship**. Can you think of more nouns that are ideas?

_____

_____

_____

_____

Math

Five lights were on in the house. James turned off 3 lights. How many lights are still on in the house?

_____ – _____ = _____

There are _____ lights still on in the house.

Language Arts

A conjunction joins two words, phrases, or sentences. Use the words in the box to complete the sentences.

and	but	so

1. Casey found a penny _____ put it in her pocket.

2. Hector wanted to wear shorts, _____ it was snowing.

3. Julia will go to bed now, _____ it is time to turn off her light.

Context Clues

Science

Fill in the blanks with words from the word bank.

bones	heart	lungs	muscles

1. Your _____ give your body its structure.

2. You use your _____ to move body parts.

3. Your _____ are used to breathe.

4. Your _____ pumps blood through your body.

Extra Credit

Circle the word that could complete both sentences.

grate	great

1. I had a _____ time at the party.

2. Katie is a _____ friend.

Math

Write the number word that describes each group.

_____

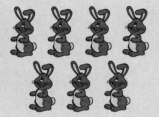
_____

Language Arts

Write a sentence to describe a teddy bear. Use two adjectives in your sentence.

_____

_____

Adjectives

Science

Think of your sense of taste and answer the questions below.

1. What is your favorite food?

_____

2. Is it bitter, salty, sweet, or sour?

_____

Extra Credit

What adjectives describe how you would feel on a hot, sunny day?

_____

_____

Math

Write 12 question marks on the lines below.

_____

_____

_____

Language Arts

Write a question mark at the end of each asking sentence.

1. Will we bake a cake

2. Do we have eggs

3. Shall we use chocolate frosting

Sentences

Science

Scientists ask many questions. Fill in the blanks with letters to complete the question words.

1. w___o

2. wh___t

3. wh___r___

4. w___e___

Extra Credit

Question words are important. They help you find information. Use each word to write a question.

Who or What? _____

Where? _____

When? _____

Why? _____

How? _____

Math

Write the word **true** or **false** on the line.

_____

$3 + 9 = 3 + 8$

Language Arts

Write an antonym for each word.

1. dangerous _____

2. colorful _____

3. careless _____

Antonyms

Science

Write the letter to match the type of motion with the picture.

1. _____   2. _____

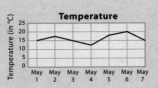

A. straight line   B. zigzag

Extra Credit

Write a sentence using the words **wet** and **dry**.

_____

_____

_____

Math

This is a verb web. Write six verbs on the lines.

_____   _____

_____ (Verbs) _____

_____   _____

Language Arts

Circle each verb.

1. Yosef rides his bike.

2. Claire holds the fork.

3. Mia smells the food.

4. Taylor sees her mom.

Verbs

Science

Use a verb, or action word, to tell how each animal moves.

1. snake _____

2. bird _____

3. kangaroo _____

4. cheetah _____

Extra Credit

Some verbs are action words. They show movement. Write three action verbs.

1. _____

2. _____

3. _____

Math

Write the correct answer to each question.

9 + 1 is the same as

5 + _____

7 + 2 is the same as

1 + _____

Language Arts

Write a synonym for each word.

1. center _____

2. kind _____

3. begin _____

Synonyms

Science

Circle the correct answer.

Another word for animal home is _____.

hamster   habitat   heart

Extra Credit

Can you think of synonyms for these words?

1. sniff _____

2. exit _____

3. sack _____

Math

Circle the shape whose name has the **long u** sound.

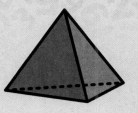

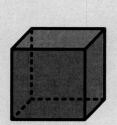

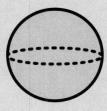

Language Arts

Several vowel pairs can make the **long u** sound. Complete each word with the correct letters.

ue	oo	ew

1. The bl_____ sky was beautiful.

2. The tree has r_____ts.

3. The breeze bl_____ the trees.

Vowel Sounds

Science

Write the missing vowels in each sentence.

1. W___t___r changes the shapes of the land.

2. A glacier is a large mass of ___ce.

3. W___nd can be a powerful force.

Extra Credit

What vowel sounds do you hear in your name?

_____

What vowel sounds do you hear in your best friend's name?

_____

Math

Write a sentence with each homophone. Circle the homophone that is a number word.

1. one _____

2. won _____

Language Arts

Draw lines to match the homophones.

aunt   flour

flower   dear

deer   ant

Homophones

Science

Write a homophone for each word. Circle the homophone in each pair that is an animal name.

1. hare _____

2. bare _____

Extra Credit

Write a silly sentence with one pair of homophones.

Example: The little hare had long pink hair.

_____

_____

Math

Jose has 3 erasers. His friend gives him 1 more. How many erasers does Jose have?

Jose has _____ erasers.

Language Arts

A chimpanzee was caught in a trap in 2007. She was very young. Her name was Mugu Moja. She lived in Africa. The trap was around her leg. A man took the trap off of her. Her leg was hurt. A doctor took care of her.

1. Who is the main topic of the story?

   _____

2. What type of animal is she?

   _____

3. Where does she live?

   _____

Reading Comprehension

Science

Do you see a shadow in front of you? If you do, then the light is behind you. Is your shadow behind you? Then, the light is in front of you. Shadows are dark, but they are made by light.

1. Where is the light if the shadow is in front of you? _____

2. Where is the light if the shadow is behind you? _____

Extra Credit

What else did you learn about Mugu Moja from the story above?

_____

_____

Math

Circle the five nouns.

said   with   hat

kick   pup   bib   write

can   bag   sweep

Language Arts

Make each noun plural by adding **-s** to the end.

top___

number___

lake___

car___

Nouns

Science

Sort these nouns from lightest to heaviest: **brick, candy bar, feather,** and **car**.

1. _____

2. _____

3. _____

4. _____

Extra Credit

Plural means more than one. Adding an -s to a noun can make it mean more than one. Some nouns stay the same when they are plural—like sheep! Write three plural nouns.

1. _____

2. _____

3. _____

Math

Mischa has 11 dolls. She gave 2 dolls to her granddaughter. How many dolls does Mischa have left?

_____ − _____ = _____

Mischa has _____ dolls left.

Language Arts

To, **two**, and **too** each mean something different. Use the correct word in each sentence.

1. We went _____ the house.

2. There are _____ kids in the yard.

3. We will play at the house _____.

Context Clues

Science

Fill in the blanks with the words from the word box.

beak	hide	roots

1. A snowshoe hare's white fur helps it to camouflage, or _____, in the snow.

2. A hummingbird's long _____ helps it collect nectar from flowers.

3. Tree adapt to long periods without water by growing long _____.

Extra Credit

Circle the word that could complete both sentences.

where	wear

1. _____ is my jacket?

2. I told Mom _____ to find the puppy.

Math

Write the number word that describes each group.

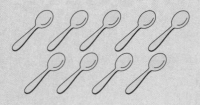

 _____

Language Arts

Write three sentences that describe the giraffe. The first sentence has been started for you.

1. The giraffe has a _____ neck.

2. _____
   _____

3. _____
   _____

Adjectives

Science

Think of your sense of taste and answer the questions below.

1. What is your least favorite food?

   _____

2. Is it bitter, salty, sweet, or sour?

   _____

Extra Credit

What are three words that describe your favorite animal?

1. _____

2. _____

3. _____

Math

Write 14 question marks on the lines below.

_____

_____

_____

Language Arts

Write a question mark at the end of each asking sentence.

1. When will Ryan get home

2. Where is he

3. Why is he late

Sentences

Science

Scientists ask many questions. Fill in the blanks with letters to complete the question words.

1. h___ ___

2. w___y

3. wh___ch

Extra Credit

Write two questions that you would ask your favorite teacher.

1. _____

_____

2. _____

_____

Math

Write a verb to complete each sentence. Then, solve the problem.

Jason _____ 5 apple pies. Then, Jason

_____ 4 more apple pies.

How many pies in all?

____

Language Arts

Circle each verb.

1. Cara calls for her dad.

2. Eric looks outside.

3. Jessi sits in her seat.

4. Victor plays ball.

Verbs

Science

Circle the animals that hatch from eggs.

birds

turtles

people

dogs

Extra Credit

Think of three verbs that would tell about the way a horse moves.

1. _____

2. _____

3. _____

Math

Prefix + Word = Meaning

Write the meaning of each new word.

1. re + write = _____

2. pre + game = _____

3. un + welcome = _____

Language Arts

Re- means **again**. Write what each word means. The first one has been done for you.

1. retest   test again

2. retell   _____

3. repack   _____

4. repay   _____

Prefixes

Science

Write the foods in the correct box.

potato	chips	apple	candy
carrots	lettuce	cookies	

Healthy	Unhealthy

Extra Credit

Name three words that have the prefix un-, which means **not**.

1. _____

2. _____

3. _____

Math

Count the objects to help you solve the problem.

3 + 2 = _____

What short vowel sound do you hear in the word **fish**?

_____

Language Arts

Circle the picture whose name has the **short i** sound.

Vowel Sounds

Science

Fill in the missing vowels.

1. A be___k___r can hold and measure liquids.

2. The sun provides l___ght to help us see.

Extra Credit

Can you think of two words that rhyme with **fish**?

1. _____

2. _____

Math

Add the suffix -ful to each word. Then, write the word.

1. thank + ful = _____

2. harm + ful = _____

3. peace + ful = _____

4. truth + ful = _____

Language Arts

Write what each word means. The first one has been done for you.

1. graceful   full of grace

2. cheerful   _____

3. painful   _____

4. useful   _____

Suffixes

Science

1. Name one way the sun is helpful to plants or animals.

_____

_____

2. Name one way the sun is harmful to plants or animals.

_____

_____

Extra Credit

A suffix is a word part. It is at the end of a word. The suffix -ful means **full of**. Write three words that end in -ful.

1. _____

2. _____

3. _____

Math

Write a sentence with each homophone. Circle the homophone that is a number word.

1. ate

   _____

2. eight

   _____

Language Arts

Draw lines to match the homophones.

there   pare

where   wear

pear   their

Homophones

Science

Write the correct homophone to complete the sentence.

here   hear

We use our ears to _____ and our eyes to see.

Extra Credit

Write a funny sentence using the homophones **eye** and **I**.

_____

_____

_____

Math

Tyrone caught 11 fish one day. The next day, he caught 9 more fish. How many fish did Tyrone catch in all?

Tyrone caught _____ fish.

Language Arts

Read the story and answer the questions.

Ahmad is in a big room. It is on the top floor of his house. It is his attic. It is dark and dusty. Webs are in the corners. Ahmad finds a light. He pulls the string.

1. Where is Ahmad? _____

2. What is the attic like? _____

3. What are in the corners? _____

4. What did Ahmad find? _____

Reading Comprehension

Science

Trash is in landfills. A landfill is a big pile of waste. Paper is in landfills. Plastic is in landfills. Landfills make gas. We can recycle. When we recycle, the waste is used again. We do not have to put all trash in landfills.

1. What is a landfill?

_____

2. What is in landfills?

_____

3. What happens when we recycle?

_____

Extra Credit

Tell what happened during your favorite part of your favorite movie.

_____

_____

_____

_____

Math

Circle the five nouns.

walk   and   shoe

spin   kitten   shirt   draw

would   backpack   cup

Language Arts

Capitalize each proper noun.

paul _____

karen _____

norwalk _____

washington _____

Nouns

Science

Use the nouns from the word box to complete the sentences.

turtle	dog	shark

1. A _____ is a mammal.

2. A _____ is a reptile.

3. A _____ is a fish.

Extra Credit

Make a list of five proper nouns. Remember to capitalize the first letter of each.

1. _____

2. _____

3. _____

4. _____

5. _____

Math

Jack swam for 3 hours on Saturday. He swam for 4 more hours on Sunday. How many total hours did Jack swim on Saturday and Sunday?

Jack swam _____ total hours on Saturday and Sunday.

Language Arts

Write the steps to make a sandwich.

1. First, I get a piece of _____ . It is on the bottom.

2. Then, _____
   _____ .

3. Next, _____
   _____ .

4. Last, I put another piece of _____ on top.

Context Clues

Science

Fill in the missing letters. Use the clues to figure out the three forms of energy.

1. L___gh___ energy comes from the sun and helps us to see objects.

2. Hea___ energy gives us warmth. It comes from sources like the sun and fire.

3. S___ ___nd energy comes from vibrations. We use our ears to hear it.

Extra Credit

Circle the word that could complete both sentences.

mouse   moose

1. The _____ for my computer is broken.

2. Eric screamed when the tiny _____ ran into the hole.

Math

Label the crayons **small**, **smaller**, **smallest**.

_____

_____

_____

Language Arts

Some words are strong adjectives. Make the adjective stronger.

big = huge

small = _____

Adjectives

Science

Think of your sense of touch and answer the questions below.

1. Name something that feels hot.

_____

2. Name something that feels cold.

_____

Extra Credit

Write three adjectives that describe your favorite kind of pizza.

1. _____

2. _____

3. _____

Math

Write the correct answer to each number sentence.

$10 - 2 = $ _____

$5 + 4 = $ _____

$2 + 1 = $ _____

$3 - 3 = $ _____

Language Arts

Read each sentence. Put a period at the end if the sentence tells something. Put a question mark at the end if the sentence asks a question.

1. Where are you going

2. I see a red truck

3. Lee is in the car

Sentences

Science

Write a sentence that tells one way that you can stay healthy.

_____

_____

_____

Extra Credit

Your school plans to start a school garden. Write two questions you might have before you start.

1. _____

_____

2. _____

_____

Math

Circle each verb.

1. Kevin runs to school.

2. Zach jumps rope.

3. Vanessa finds her doll.

4. Molly lifts the blinds.

How many verbs did you find in all? _____

Language Arts

Write the present and future form of each verb.

1. Past: kicked

   Present: _____

   Future: _____ _____

2. Past: baked

   Present: _____

   Future: _____

   _____

Verbs

Science

Circle the animals that fly.

bats

whales

birds

people

Extra Credit

A verb is an action word. It can be in the past, present, or future tense. Write the past and future forms of the verb **play**.

Past: _____

Future: _____

Math

Write the correct answer to complete each number sentence.

$5 + \underline{\hspace{1cm}} = 9$

$9 - \underline{\hspace{1cm}} = 3$

$4 + \underline{\hspace{1cm}} = 7$

$8 - \underline{\hspace{1cm}} = 1$

Language Arts

Write the first words of each sentence. Use a capital letter.

1. (kit) _____ will go to the store.

2. (please) _____ look at the map.

3. (they) _____ will play.

Sentences

Science

In a complete sentence, name three ways humans or animals use water.

_____

_____

_____

_____

Extra Credit

Write two sentences about a time when you felt proud.

_____

_____

_____

_____

Math

Write three words that have short vowel sounds.

1. _____

2. _____

3. _____

Language Arts

Circle the picture whose name has the **short o** sound.

Vowel Sounds

Science

Fill in the missing vowels.

1. The s___n provides heat.

2. Plants use energy from the sun, along with air and water, to make f___ ___d.

Extra Credit

Say your teacher's name. What vowel sounds do you hear in his or her name?

_____

_____

Math

Add the suffix -er to each word. Then, write the word.

1. teach + er = _____

2. walk + er = _____

3. think + er = _____

4. sweep + er = _____

Language Arts

Write what each word means. The first one has been done for you.

1. careful   full of care

2. joyful   _____

3. fearful   _____

4. colorful   _____

Suffixes

Science

Find and circle the suffix -ful in each sentence below.

1. Ellie was very careful when she planted the seeds.

2. She is hopeful her pumpkins will grow.

Extra Credit

What does the suffix -ful mean?

_____

Write a word with the -ful suffix.

_____

Math

Write a sentence with each homophone. Circle the homophone that is a number word.

1. four

_____

2. for

_____

Language Arts

Write the correct word to complete each sentence.

sun   son

1. My _____ was born in September.

2. I got too much _____ at the beach.

Homophones

Science

Write the correct homophone to complete the sentence.

flower   flour

A _____ has a stem, leaves, and petals.

Extra Credit

Write a funny sentence using the homophones **plain** and **plane**.

_____

_____

_____

Math

Leslie buys 12 gallons of lemonade for the party. She serves 9 gallons of lemonade during the party. How many gallons of lemonade does Leslie have left?

Leslie has _____ gallons of lemonade left.

Language Arts

Read the story and answer the questions.

Josie and Paws play with yarn. Josie tosses up the yarn. Paws jumps for it! Josie rolls it on the floor. Paws gets ready to pounce! Josie and Paws are good friends. Paws likes it when Josie brushes his fur. It makes Paws purr.

1. Who is Paws? _____

2. What does Josie do with the yarn?

   _____

3. What does Paws like?

   _____

   _____

Reading Comprehension

Science

Read the paragraph and answer the questions.

It is important to take care of the planet. Too much trash and gas could harm Earth. It will get warmer. Global warming means that the planet is getting warmer.

1. What do we need to take of?

   _____

2. What could harm Earth? _____

   _____

3. What is global warming? _____

   _____

Extra Credit

Think of your favorite fairy tale and retell the story to a friend. Remember to include the beginning, the middle, and the end of the story.

_____

_____

_____

_____

Math

Circle five proper nouns.

cat   Jamie   Wednesday

tomorrow   desk   January

Ohio   papers   David

Language Arts

Rewrite each word, beginning with a capital letter.

1. sunday _____

2. may _____

3. september _____

4. saturday _____

Nouns

Science

Use the nouns from the word box to complete the sentences.

penguin	frog	koala

1. A _____ is a mammal.

2. A _____ is an amphibian.

3. A _____ is a bird.

Extra Credit

Make a list of five different nouns. Then, on a seperate piece of paper, write a story including all of the nouns on your list.

1. _____

2. _____

3. _____

4. _____

5. _____

Math

We saw 16 dolphins playing in the water. We saw 3 swim away. How many dolphins are left playing in the water?

_____ dolphins are left playing in the water.

Language Arts

Write about what you want to do. Complete each sentence.

First Sentence: I want to _____
_____.

Detail Sentence: I want to do this because _____.

Detail Sentence: When I _____, I will feel _____.

Last sentence:

I cannot wait to _____
_____
_____.

Context Clues

Science

Fill in the blanks using words from the word bank.

| bee | birds | flowers | skunks |

1. A _____ has a stinger to protect it from predators.

2. _____ have colorful petals to attract insects.

3. Some _____ have strong beaks to crack open seeds.

4. _____ are black and white to warn other animals.

Extra Credit

Think of a word that could complete both sentences.

1. _____ you like some tea?

2. I knew Jack _____ win the race.

Math

Number the objects as follows:

1 = long
2 = medium
3 = short

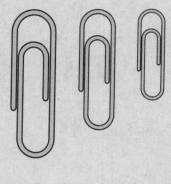

___   ___   ___

Language Arts

Make each adjective stronger.

warm = hot

cold = _____

Adjectives

Science

Think of your sense of touch and answer the questions below.

1. Name something that feels prickly.

   _____

2. Name something that feels smooth.

   _____

Extra Credit

Write three adjectives that describe a campfire.

1. _____

2. _____

3. _____

Math

Write the correct answer to complete each number sentence.

$8 - 3 =$ _____

$10 + 2 =$ _____

$4 - 1 =$ _____

$5 + 6 =$ _____

Language Arts

Add an exclamation point at the end of each sentence.

1. That is great ___

2. I am happy for you ___

3. This is wild ___

Sentences

Science

Draw a picture of your favorite fruit. Then, write a sentence that describes the fruit.

_____

_____

Extra Credit

An exclamatory sentence shows a lot of feeling. Write an exclamatory sentence about a time you were excited by something.

_____

_____

_____

Math

Circle each verb.

1. Rusty makes cookies.

2. Jeff sells apples.

3. Nora cleans her room.

4. Mariah swims in the pool.

How many verbs did you find in all? _____

Language Arts

Write the present and future form of each verb.

1. Past: wanted

   Present: _____

   Future: _____ _____

2. Past: laughed

   Present: _____

   Future: _____

   _____

Verbs

Science

Write a verb to complete the sentence.

Scientists _____ goggles to protect their eyes.

Extra Credit

Think of three verbs. Write each of them in past, present, and future form.

1. _____, _____, _____

2. _____, _____, _____

3. _____, _____, _____

Consonant Blends

Math

Write three words that begin with the consonant blend **bl**.

1. _____

2. _____

3. _____

Language Arts

Circle the blend in each word.

1. blue

2. blip

3. blot

4. blur

Consonant Blends

Science

Circle the consonant blend or blends in each animal name.

1. snake

2. clam

3. dragonfly

4. frog

Extra Credit

A consonant blend is when two consonants appear together. A blend can be at the beginning or the end of a word. Write three words that have consonant blends.

1. _____

2. _____

3. _____

Math

Draw lines to match the words that rhyme. Listen for the vowel sounds.

five   blue

two   tree

three   hive

Language Arts

Circle the correct words.

1. cit or cat ?

2. buth or bath ?

3. fish or fash ?

4. swom or swim ?

Vowel Sounds

Science

Fill in the missing letters to complete each sentence.

1. Water that falls from clouds as a liquid is called r___ ___n.

2. Water that falls from clouds as a crystal is called sn___ ___.

Extra Credit

Think of three words that rhyme with **coat**.

1. _____

2. _____

3. _____

Math

Add the suffix -ful to each word. Then, write the word.

1. care + ful = _____

2. joy + ful = _____

3. color + ful = _____

4. fear + ful = _____

Language Arts

Write what each word means. The first one has been done for you.

1. teacher   one who teaches

2. server   _____

3. diver   _____

4. baker   _____

Suffixes

Science

Find and circle the suffix -er in each sentence below.

1. My science teacher taught us about the desert habitat.

2. I am going to be her helper with the lesson about deserts.

Extra Credit

What does the suffix -er mean? Think of a word with the -er suffix.

_____

Write a word with the -er suffix.

_____

Math

Write the word **true** or **false** on the line.

_____

9 – 3 = 8 – 2

Language Arts

Write an antonym for each word.

1. happy _____

2. left _____

3. high _____

4. light _____

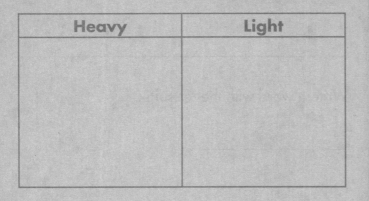

Antonyms

Science

Fill in the chart with six items you can observe at home or in your classroom.

Heavy	Light

Extra Credit

Think of an antonym pair. Write a silly sentence using both words.

_____

_____

_____

Math

Circle the digraphs in the words below.

which   wish

chug   while   shoe

this   that

How many digraphs did you circle? _____

Language Arts

Add **sh** to complete each word. Write the word.

1. _____ip   _____

2. di_____   _____

3. _____in   _____

Consonant Digraphs

Science

Circle the correct answer.

What is the name of the science tool used to measure temperature?

A. microscope
B. telescope
C. thermometer

Write the digraph found in the answer that you circled.

_____

Extra Credit

A digraph is two letters that make a new sound. **sh**, **ch**, **wh**, and **th** are all digraphs. Write three words that have digraphs.

1. _____

2. _____

3. _____

Math

Write four plural nouns.

1. _____

2. _____

3. _____

4. _____

Language Arts

Capitalize each proper noun.

pascal _____

virginia _____

walsh _____

utah _____

Nouns

Science

Matter can have different textures. Write a noun to go with each description.

1. Name an object that is bumpy.

   _____

2. Name an object that is smooth.

   _____

3. Name an object that is squishy.

   _____

4. Name an object that is rough.

   _____

Extra Credit

Write a sentence that contains a proper noun.

_____

_____

_____

Math

Lucy has some marbles in her pocket. Eight of the marbles in her pocket are red. The other 12 marbles in her pocket are black. How many marbles does Lucy have in all?

Lucy has _____ marbles in all.

Language Arts

Use a word from the word box to complete each sentence.

dirty	fierce	playful	delicious

1. The fresh bread is _____.

2. The kitten is _____.

3. The lion is _____.

4. The garbage pail is _____.

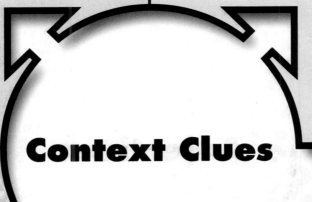

Context Clues

Science

Circle the correct word to complete each sentence.

1. Earth's surface is mostly made up of _____ (land, water).

2. Most of Earth's water is _____ (salty, freshwater).

3. Some of Earth's water cannot be used because it is _____ (frozen, fresh).

4. Water found beneath Earth's surface is called _____ (groundwater, tap water).

Extra Credit

Write a word that could complete both sentences.

1. Have you heard the _____ of the brave princess?

2. Cinderella is my favorite fairy _____.

Math

Number the objects as follows:

1 = long
2 = medium
3 = short

_____   _____   _____

Language Arts

Some words are strong adjectives. Make the adjective stronger.

soft = fluffy

large = _____

Adjectives

Science

Fill in the chart with adjectives.

Words Describing Your Favorite Fruit	Words Describing Your Least Favorite Fruit

Extra Credit

Write four adjectives to describe a dragon.

1. _____

2. _____

3. _____

4. _____

Math

Write the same verb in each blank to complete the story problem. Then, write the answer.

Sally _____ 2 flowers. She _____ 2 more flowers. How many flowers does she have in all?

Sally has _____ flowers.

Language Arts

Write two sentences. Each one should have a verb.

1. _____

_____

2. _____

_____

Verbs

Science

Circle the correct answer.

1. Water becomes a solid when it _____.

   A. evaporates
   B. freezes
   C. melts

2. Ice becomes a liquid when it _____.

   A. evaporates
   B. freezes
   C. melts

Extra Credit

Think of three action words that could tell about a basketball game.

1. _____

2. _____

3. _____

Math

Miranda orders 17 scarves. Twelve scarves come in the mail on Monday. How many more scarves still need to come?

_____ more scarves still need to come.

Language Arts

Use a word from the word box to complete each sentence.

| lion   mouse   dog   wolf |

1. The _____ roared.

2. The _____ barked.

3. The _____ squeaked.

4. The _____ howled.

Context Clues

Science

Fill in the blanks with words from the word bank.

| down   Earth   gravity   moon |

1. _____ is a force that pulls objects toward the center of _____.

2. Because of gravity, what goes up must come _____.

3. The _____ revolves around Earth because of gravity.

Extra Credit

Think of a word that could complete both sentences.

1. That is _____ camper.

2. I want to borrow _____ football.

Consonant Blends

Math

Write three words that begin with the consonant blend **fl**.

1. _____

2. _____

3. _____

Language Arts

Circle the blend in each word.

1. fry

2. frown

3. from

4. frog

Consonant Blends

Science

Circle the consonant blend or blends in each word below.

tree

flower

plant

forest

Extra Credit

Make a list of ten different consonant blends.

_____ _____

_____ _____

_____ _____

_____ _____

_____ _____

Math

Count from one to twenty. Every time you hear a long vowel sound, clap.

Language Arts

Circle the correct words.

1. pind or pond ?

2. mop or mup ?

3. ap or up ?

4. rin or run ?

Vowel Sounds

Science

Fill in the missing letters to complete each sentence.

1. Tiny drops of w___t___r form clouds.

2. Falling water collects in str___ ___ms and other bodies of water.

Extra Credit

Think of three words that rhyme with **cute**.

1. _____

2. _____

3. _____

Math

Write the word **true** or **false** on the line.

true

$5 + 6 = 2 + 9$

Language Arts

Write an antonym for each word.

1. night _____

2. hard _____

3. start _____

Antonyms

Science

Write the words from the word bank in the correct spaces. Some words may be used more than once.

bat	butterfly	cardinal	moon
	owl	stars	sun

Things I Can See During the Day	Things I Can See at Night

Extra Credit

Look around. What is above your head? What is below your feet?

_____

_____

_____

_____

Math

Number words are adjectives because they tell how many.

You have 2 bones in each thumb and 3 bones in each of your other fingers.

1. How many bones are in one hand? _____

2. How many bones are in both hands? _____

Language Arts

Write a word to describe a ball.

_____

Write a word to describe a flower.

_____

Write a word to describe a slide.

_____

Adjectives

Science

Write two adjectives that describe the pond habitat.

_____

_____

Extra Credit

Write four adjectives to describe a space creature.

1.  _____

2. _____

3. _____

4. _____

Math Skills Introduction

This Math section will address the following skills that first graders need to know:

Shapes
First graders will learn to reason with two-dimensional shapes and distinguish between their attributes. For example, first graders know that triangles have three sides and squares have four sides. They will also begin exploring three-dimensional shapes, such as cubes, pyramids, and spheres.

Number Words
First graders will practice writing and identifying number words in addition to numerals, such as **one**, **two**, and **three**.

Addition
Addition means "putting together" or adding two or more numbers to find the sum. For example, **12 + 3 = 15**. The answer in an addition problem is called the **sum**. The two numbers being added together are called the **addends**. For example, **addend + addend = sum**.

Subtraction
Subtraction means "taking away" or subtracting one number from another to find the difference. For example, **15 − 11 = 4**. The answer in a subtraction problem is called the **difference**. The number that is being subtracted from is called the **minuend**, and the number being subtracted is called the **subtrahend**. For example, **minuend − subtrahend = difference**.

Time
Time can be measured in seconds, minutes, hours, days, weeks, months, and years The short hand on a clock is the hour hand. The long hand on a clock is the minute hand. It shows the number of minutes after the hour. For example, if the hour hand is pointing to the 4 and the minute hand is pointing to the 6, the time would be **4:30**. First graders will be asked to tell and write time to the hour and half-hour.

Greater Than/Less Than
First graders will be asked to compare two two-digit numbers, determining which is larger and which is smaller. The numbers can be compared using the symbols < and >. For example, **98 < 99** and **43 > 24**.

Place Value

The place value of a numeral is shown by where it is in the number. For example, in the number **34**, 3 is **tens**, and 4 is **ones**.

Fractions

A fraction is a number that names part of a whole number, such as $\frac{1}{2}$ or $\frac{1}{4}$. If you divide something in half ($\frac{1}{2}$), you divide it into two equal parts. If you divide something in fourths ($\frac{1}{4}$), you divide it into four equal parts. First graders will work with circles and rectangles that are divided into two and four equal portions, describing the fractions using words such as **halves**, **fourths**, and **quarters**.

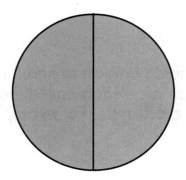 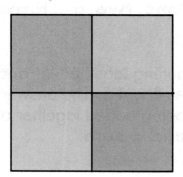

Measurement

First graders will be asked to order three objects by length, and to compare the lengths of two objects indirectly by using a third object.

Graphing

First graders will use graphing to analyze and interpret information with up to three categories.

Sequencing Numbers

Sequencing numbers means putting them in the correct order, whether consecutively or otherwise. For example, **3, 4, 5**, and **28, 37, 64** are both series of numbers in the correct sequence.

Math

How many cubes long is the pencil?

The pencil is _____ cubes long.

Language Arts

Sally is baking a cake. Circle the measuring tools that she might use.

ruler   teaspoon   measuring cups

scale   thermometer

Measurement

Science

How many paper clips long is the leaf?

_____ paper clips

Extra Credit

How tall are you? How many feet? How many inches?

_____

_____

_____

Math

Write the number for each number word.

ten _____

six _____

twelve _____

Language Arts

Write a sentence using each number word.

one five

1. _____

   _____

2. _____

   _____

Number Words

Science

Write a number word to complete each sentence.

Object	Hypothesis: Will it sink or float?	Results
penny	float	sink
sponge	float	float
marble	sink	sink

1. How many objects did the student think would float? _____

2. How many objects did the student think would sink? _____

Extra Credit

Next time you are at the grocery store, look around and see how many number words you can spy.

Math

Count the objects to help you solve the problem.

$4 + 1 = $ _____

Language Arts

There were 4 fish in the water. Two more fish came. How many fish were in the water altogether?

_____ + _____ = _____

Addition

Science

Circle the correct answer.

Most mammals have 4 legs. Spiders have 8 legs. So, 2 mammals and 1 spider would have _____ legs altogether.

A. 12
B. 14
C. 16
D. 18

Extra Credit

The answer in an addition problem is called the **sum**. The two numbers being added together are called the **addends**.

addend + addend = sum

Write two addends and a sum.

_____

Math

Write the time shown on the clock.

_____

Language Arts

Circle the correct answer.

Jeannette started her homework at 5:00. She finished at 6:00. How long did it take Jeannette to do her homework?

A. two hours
B. half an hour
C. one hour

Time

Science

Circle the best answer.

Amount of time from 6:00 a.m. to 6:00 the next morning

A. 24 hours
B. 24 seconds
C. 24 minutes

Extra Credit

Find a clock. What time is it now? What time will it be in one hour?

_____

_____

Math

Count the objects to help you solve the problem.

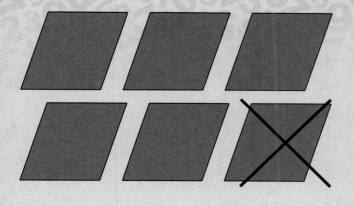

_____ – _____ = _____

Language Arts

Leo bought 15 stamps. He used 10 stamps. How many stamps does Leo have left?

Leo has _____ stamps left.

Subtraction

Science

Robin observed the animals in her backyard. She saw 4 squirrels and 8 birds. How many more birds than squirrels did Robin see?

Write a number sentence to show how to find the answer.

_____

Extra Credit

Fill in the missing subtraction facts.

20 – 0 = _____   20 – 6 = _____

20 – 1 = 19   20 – 7 = 13

20 – _____ = 18   20 – _____ = 12

20 – 3 = 17   20 – 9 = 11

_____ – 4 = 16   _____ – 10 = 10

20 – 5 = 15

Math

Circle the square.

Language Arts

Circle the names of the shapes that have four sides.

A. circle
B. square
C. triangle
D. rectangle

Shapes

Science

Circle which object can move faster when pushed down a hill.

sphere

cube

Extra Credit

Look around the room. How many squares can you find?

_____

Draw your own square in the space below.

Math

Write <, >, or = to make the statement true.

40 ◯ 37

11 ◯ 12

15 ◯ 21

32 ◯ 29

Language Arts

Fill in the blank with the correct answer.

Eleven is _____ twelve.

greater than   less than

Greater Than/ Less Than

Science

Use the chart to answer the questions. Show each answer as a number sentence using <, >, or =.

Animal	Number of Permanent Teeth
human	32
cat	30
dog	42
pig	44

Do humans have more or less permanent teeth than cats? _____ ◯ _____

Extra Credit

Write your own number sentence using < or > to show how old you are now and how old you were a year ago.

_____

Math

Circle each set of 10 objects. Write the total amount of tens and ones.

_____ tens

_____ ones

Language Arts

Write the words **tens** and **ones** to show the value of the number.

60

6 _____

0 _____

Place Value

Science

Fill in the chart to show the number values.

Number	Tens	Ones
82	8	2
65		
24		

Extra Credit

How many groups of ten are there in the number **20**?

_____

How many groups of 10 are there in the number **90**?

_____

Math

Draw lines to show how you and 3 friends can equally share this graham cracker.

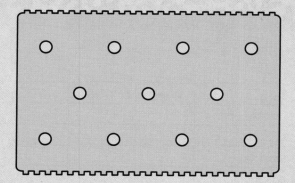

Language Arts

Circle the correct answer.

If you cut something in half, then you will have two _____ parts.

   A. different
   B. equal
   C. bigger

Fractions

Science

Color half of the bat black and half of the bat green.

Extra Credit

Fractions show parts of things. When something is divided in half, it has two equal parts.

Draw a line to divide the circle in half.

Math

Ask 7 classmates which sport they like best. In the table below, make a tally mark beside the sport each one likes best.

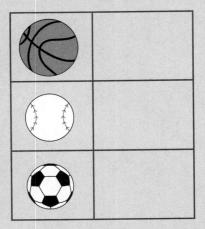

Language Arts

Insects are bugs. Some bugs are alike. Some are different. Look at the table. Write an X in the box if the bug has wings. Write an X in the box if it has six legs. Write an X in the box if it has more than six legs.

Bug	Wings	Six Legs	> Six Legs
grasshopper			
ant			
ladybug			
caterpillar			

Graphing

Science

Use the graph to answer the question.

Heights of Students' Plants in Ms. Chung's Class

Height (in cm)

Thomas   Jason   Sarah   Maggie   Tyrone

Students' Plants

What are the students observing?

Extra Credit

Complete the right side of the chart below.

My Favorites	
Dinner	
Dessert	
Animal	
Book	

Math

How many paper clips long is the screwdriver?

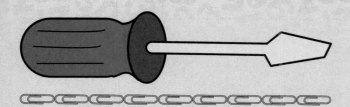

The screwdriver is _____ paper clips long.

Language Arts

What is the name of the science tool used to view tiny objects?

A. microscope
B. telescope
C. thermometer

Measurement

Science

How many paper clips long is the pencil?

_____ paper clips

Extra Credit

Use a ruler to measure your hand and foot. How long is your hand?

_____

How long is your foot?

_____

Math

Write the number for each number word.

eleven _____

three _____

nine _____

Language Arts

Write a sentence using each number word.

two   ten

1. _____

   _____

2. _____

   _____

Number Words

Science

Write the correct number word to complete each sentence.

three   eight

A caterpillar is about _____ inches long.

A car is about _____ feet long.

Extra Credit

Write the number words in order from one to ten.

_____, _____, _____,

_____, _____, _____,

_____, _____, _____,

_____

Math

Write the correct answer to each problem.

$$3 + 4$$

$$4 + 2$$

$$6 + 2$$

$$8 + 1$$

$$2 + 3$$

$$4 + 4$$

Language Arts

A gardener planted 7 trees in one row. He planted 12 trees in another row. How many trees did he plant in all? Write the correct number word to answer the question.

The gardener planted _____ trees in all.

Addition

Science

Jason collected 10 caterpillars. Brendon collected 8 caterpillars. How many caterpillars in all?

_____

Extra Credit

Fill in the missing addition facts.

$10 + 1 = $ _____ $10 + 6 = 16$

$10 + 2 = 12$ $10 + 7 = $ _____

_____ $ + 3 = 13$ _____ $ + 8 = 18$

$10 + 4 = $ _____ $10 + $ _____ $ = 19$

$10 + $ _____ $ = 15$ $10 + 10 = 20$

Math

Write the time shown on the clock.

_____

Language Arts

Circle the correct answer.

Ellie walked home from school. She left school at 3:00. She got home at 3:30. How long did it take Ellie to walk home?

A. 20 minutes
B. 30 minutes
C. 40 minutes

Time

Science

Circle the best answer.

Time it takes to wash your hands

A. 30 seconds
B. 30 minutes
C. 30 hours

Extra Credit

The short hand on a clock is the hour hand. Look at a clock. What number is the hour hand pointing to?

_____

Math

$$\begin{array}{r} 8 \\ -\ 6 \\ \hline \end{array} \qquad \begin{array}{r} 5 \\ -\ 2 \\ \hline \end{array}$$

$$\begin{array}{r} 7 \\ -\ 1 \\ \hline \end{array} \qquad \begin{array}{r} 4 \\ -\ 3 \\ \hline \end{array}$$

$$\begin{array}{r} 9 \\ -\ 2 \\ \hline \end{array} \qquad \begin{array}{r} 6 \\ -\ 0 \\ \hline \end{array}$$

Language Arts

Mrs. Freeman bakes 16 cupcakes. She sells 4. How many cupcakes does Mrs. Freeman have left? Write the correct number word to answer the question.

Mrs. Freeman has _____ cupcakes left.

Subtraction

Science

Fifteen birds are in a tree. Nine fly away. How many birds are left?

_____ birds are left.

Extra Credit

Fill in the missing subtraction facts.

$10 - 0 = 10$ $10 - 6 = $ ____

$10 - 1 = $ ____ $10 - 7 = 3$

$10 - 2 = 8$ $10 - $ ____ $= 2$

$10 - $ ____ $= 7$ ____ $- 9 = 1$

____ $- 4 = 6$ $10 - 10 = 0$

$10 - 5 = $ ____

Math

Name the shape you think will roll down a hill the fastest.

_____

Why?

_____

Language Arts

Circle the name of the shape that has three sides.

A. circle
B. square
C. triangle
D. rectangle

Shapes

Science

How do the hands of a clock move? Circle the correct answer.

A. round and round in a circle
B. in a straight line
C. in a zigzag pattern

Extra Credit

Look around the room. How many circles can you find?

_____

Draw your own circle in the space below.

Math

Write the number that is 10 less than the number shown.

16 _____

Write the number that is 5 less than the number shown.

14 _____

Language Arts

Fill in the blank with the correct answer.

Twenty is _____ eighteen.

greater than   less than

Greater Than/ Less Than

Science

Use the chart to answer the questions. Show each answer as a number sentence using <, >, or =.

Animal	Number of Permanent Teeth
human	32
cat	30
dog	42
pig	44

Do humans have more or less permanent teeth than pigs? _____ ◯ _____

Extra Credit

Name three numbers greater than 15, but less than 19.

_____

_____

_____

Math

Circle each set of 10 objects. Write the total amount of tens and ones.

_____ tens

_____ ones

Language Arts

Write the words **tens** and **ones** to show the value of the number.

98

9 _____

8 _____

Science

Fill in the chart to show the number values.

Number	Tens	Ones
23	2	3
40		
99		

Place Value

Extra Credit

How many groups of ten are there in the number **40**?

_____

How many groups of ten are there in the number **30**?

_____

Math

Draw lines to show how you and 3 friends can equally share this brownie.

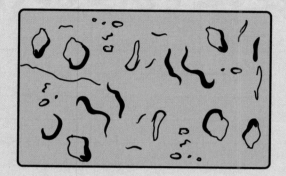

Language Arts

Circle the correct answer.

If a cake is cut into three equal parts, the cake is cut into _____.

A. halves
B. wholes
C. thirds

Fractions

Science

Color the whole circle yellow.
Color half of the square red.

Extra Credit

Gather a bowl of small objects, such as marbles or pennies. Imagine you are going to share the objects with a friend. Divide the objects into two groups so that you and your friend have the same amount.

Math

Ask 10 classmates which drink they like best. In the table below, make a tally mark beside the drink each one likes best.

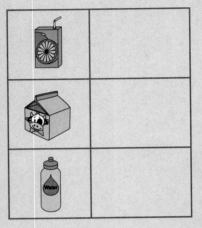

Language Arts

Write the correct types of words in each column.

NOUN	VERB	ADJECTIVE
person, place, thing, or idea	action word	describing word
apple	run	small

Graphing

Science

Use the table below to answer the questions.

Type of Seed	Seeds Left	Seeds Eaten
black oil sunflower seeds	2	8
striped sunflower seeds	5	5
safflower seeds	10	0
white millet	7	3

1. Which type of seed did the birds eat most?

   _____

2. Which type of seed did the birds eat least?

   _____

Extra Credit

Ask five people which ice cream flavor they like best. Fill in the graph to show your results.

5			
4			
3			
2			
1			
	Vanilla	Chocolate	Strawberry

What was the most popular flavor?

_____

Math

How many paper clips long is the comb?

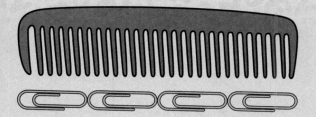

The comb is _____ paper clips long.

Language Arts

Which is the smallest? Circle the correct answer.

A. yard
B. foot
C. inch

Measurement

Science

Circle the stick that is 8 pennies long.

Extra Credit

What are three different ways that you could measure a teddy bear?

1. _____
2. _____
3. _____

Math

Draw a line to match each number word to its number.

twenty-eight   14

fourteen   5

five   28

Language Arts

Write the number and the number word three times each.

3 _____ _____ _____

three _____ _____ _____

Number Words

Science

Circle the correct answer.

How many months does it take Earth to orbit the sun?

A. ten
B. twelve
C. fourteen

Extra Credit

Write the number word for the number that comes between eight and ten.

_____

Write the number word for the number that comes between eleven and thirteen.

_____

Math

Write the correct answer to each problem.

$$\begin{array}{r} 7 \\ +\ 7 \\ \hline \end{array} \qquad \begin{array}{r} 8 \\ +\ 2 \\ \hline \end{array}$$

$$\begin{array}{r} 9 \\ +\ 3 \\ \hline \end{array} \qquad \begin{array}{r} 6 \\ +\ 5 \\ \hline \end{array}$$

$$\begin{array}{r} 5 \\ +\ 4 \\ \hline \end{array} \qquad \begin{array}{r} 10 \\ +\ 5 \\ \hline \end{array}$$

Language Arts

Write the word **true** or **false** on the line.

_____

$10 + 8 = 8 + 10$

Addition

Science

Matthew found 10 salamanders on his hike. He also spotted 5 birds. How many animals did Matthew see in all?

_____

Extra Credit

At dinner, add up the total number of knives, forks, and spoons on the table.

_____

Classroom Connections Grade 1

175

Math

Write the time shown on the clock.

_____

Language Arts

Marian ran a race in twelve minutes. The second time she ran the race, she finished two minutes faster. How long did it take Marian to run the second time? Use a number word to write the correct answer.

_____

Time

Science

Circle the best answer.

How often the garbage truck comes to your house

A. every day
B. every week
C. every month

Extra Credit

The long hand on a clock is the minute hand. It shows the number of minutes after the hour. Draw a clock that shows 7:00.

Math

Count the objects to help you solve the problem.

_____ − _____ = _____

Language Arts

Mia picked 10 tomatoes. She gave 3 to her neighbor. How many tomatoes does Mia have left? Use a number word to write the correct answer.

Mia has _____ tomatoes left.

Subtraction

Science

In the morning, the temperature was 14°C. By afternoon, the temperature was 20°C.

1. How many degrees did the temperature change?

   _____°C

2. How did you get your answer?

   _____

Extra Credit

Count all of the objects in your backpack. Take three of them away. How many are left?

_____

Math

Draw a square.

Language Arts

Circle the name of the shape that has two long sides and two short sides.

1. rectangle

2. square

3. triangle

4. circle

Shapes

Science

Circle the correct answer.

The moon is actually what 3-D shape?

A. circle
B. cube
C. pyramid
D. sphere

Extra Credit

Draw a car using only circles, squares, and triangles.

Math

Write <, >, or = to make the statement true.

55 ◯ 35

33 ◯ 34

45 ◯ 51

17 ◯ 15

21 ◯ 20

Language Arts

Fill in the blank with the correct answer.

Fourteen is _____ twelve.

greater than   less than

Greater Than/ Less Than

Science

Circle the insect that has the greatest length.

luna moth = 80 mm

bumblebee = 12 mm

flea = 2 mm

grasshopper = 40 mm

Extra Credit

Write the number that is greater than 15, but less than 17.

_____

Write the number that is greater than nineteen, but less than twenty-one.

_____

Math

Circle each set of 10 objects. Write the total amount of tens and ones.

_____ tens

_____ ones

Language Arts

Write the words **tens** and **ones** to show the value of the number.

72

7 _____

2 _____

Place Value

Science

Fill in the chart to show the number values.

Number	Tens	Ones
55	5	5
62		
81		

Extra Credit

How many groups of ten are there in the number **33**?

_____

How many groups of ten are there in the number **98**?

_____

Math

Draw a line to show how you and 1 friend can equally share this apple pie.

Language Arts

If a cupcake is cut into two equal parts, it is cut in:

A. thirds
B. whole
C. half

Fractions

Science

Color half of the triangle red and half of the triangle green.

Extra Credit

Divide this pizza into four equal parts.

Math

Ask 10 classmates what their favorite things to do on the playground are. In the table below, make a tally mark beside the thing each one likes best.

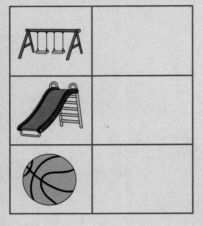

Language Arts

Complete the chart.

great	greater	greatest
long		
small		

Graphing

Science

Marcus wanted to learn more about the insects near his house. After coming up with a question, he observed the insects. Here are his notes.

Insect	Time	What It Ate
grasshopper	10:00 am	leaf
butterfly	10:05 am	nothing
grasshopper	10:30 am	nothing

What question do you think Marcus asked?

_____

_____

Extra Credit

Ask a grown-up to help you make a chart that shows the different ways you can help out at home.

Math

How many hands tall is the horse?

The horse is _____ hands tall.

Language Arts

Write the plural for each unit.

1. inch _____

2. foot _____

Measurement

Science

How many centimeters long is the stick?

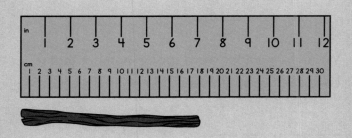

_____ cm

Extra Credit

Look around your kitchen with a grown-up. How many measuring tools can you find?

_____

Math

Draw a line to match each number word to its number.

sixteen   16

four   20

twenty   4

Language Arts

Write each number word.

16 _____

17 _____

18 _____

Number Words

Science

Write the number word that tells how many moons Earth has.

_____

Extra Credit

Write the number word for the number that comes between ten and twelve.

_____

Write the number word for the number that comes between eighteen and twenty.

_____

Math

Count the objects to help you solve the problem.

$3 + 3 =$ _____

Language Arts

Scott picks 11 apples. He picks 3 more apples. How many apples does Scott pick in all? Use a number word to write the correct answer.

Scott picks _____ apples in all.

Addition

Science

Fill in the number sentence to show the total amount of liquid in the beakers.

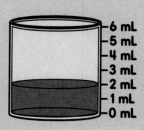

_____ + _____ = _____ mL

Extra Credit

Fill in the missing addition facts.

$11 + 0 = 11$ $11 +$ _____ $= 16$

$11 + 1 =$ _____ $11 + 6 =$ _____

$11 + 2 = 13$ _____ $+ 7 = 18$

$11 + 3 =$ _____ $11 + 8 = 19$

$11 +$ _____ $= 15$ $11 + 9 =$ _____

Math

Write the time shown on the clock.

_____

Language Arts

Write **true** or **false**.

1. _____ The sun circles around Earth to make day and night.

2. _____ Earth circles around the sun to make day and night.

Time

Science

Write a word from the word box to answer each question.

nighttime	noon

1. If it is daytime on one side of the world, it is

_____ on the other side of the

world.

2. Will you be more likely to be in school at

noon or at midnight? _____

Extra Credit

What time do you go to bed at night? What time do you wake up in the morning?

_____

_____

_____

Math

Count the objects to help you solve the problem.

_____ − _____ = _____

Language Arts

April orders 8 sandwiches. Five of the sandwiches are turkey. How many of the sandwiches are not turkey? Use a number word to write the correct answer.

_____ of the sandwiches are not turkey.

Subtraction

Science

Maggie has a rock that is 5 cm long. Tess has a rock that is 10 cm long. How much longer is Tess' rock than Maggie's?

Write a subtraction sentence to show how to find the answer.

_____ − _____ = _____ cm

Extra Credit

Write the answers to the facts.

$15 - 0 =$ _____

$15 - 1 =$ _____

$15 - 2 =$ _____

$15 - 3 =$ _____

$15 - 4 =$ _____

$15 - 5 =$ _____

Math

Draw a triangle.

Language Arts

Circle the name of the shape below.

   A. octagon

   B. square

   C. circle

   D. trapezoid

Shapes

Science

Draw lines to match the picture with the shape the moon appears to be.

    circle

    crescent (like a fingernail)

    half circle

Extra Credit

Draw a house using only shapes.

Math

Write <, >, or = to make the statement true.

28 ◯ 38

4 ◯ 14

37 ◯ 19

50 ◯ 51

81 ◯ 18

Language Arts

Fill in the blank with the correct answer.

Twenty is _____ fourteen.

greater than   less than

Greater Than/ Less Than

Science

Circle the object that has a length of less than 10 cm.

pencil = 15 cm

paper clip = 3 cm

scissors = 13 cm

Extra Credit

Write the numbers that are greater than 12 but less than 17.

_____

_____

_____

_____

Math

Write the number that is 10 less than the number shown.

86 _____

74 _____

31 _____

17 _____

59 _____

Language Arts

Write the words **tens** and **ones** to show the value of the number.

30 _____

3 _____

0 _____

Place Value

Science

Circle each set of 10 objects. Write the total amount of tens and ones.

_____ tens

_____ ones

Extra Credit

How many ones are there in the number **75**?

_____

How many tens are there in the number **61**?

_____

Math

Draw lines to show how you and 3 friends can equally share this cake.

Language Arts

Fill in the blank with the correct answer.

If you cut a pie into four equal pieces, you cut it into _____.

A. half
B. thirds
C. fourths

Fractions

Science

Color half of the acorns brown.

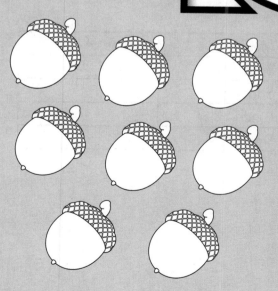

Extra Credit

Divide this cookie into two equal parts.

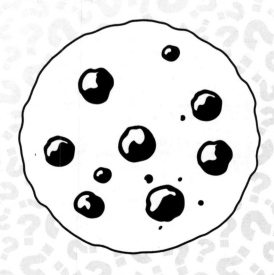

Math

Look at the tally chart. Who has the most pennies in her piggy bank?

Pennies in the Piggy Bank		
Alexa	Grace	Lynn
卌 卌 卌	卌 卌	卌 卌 卌 卌 卌 卌 卌 卌卌

_____ has the most pennies in her piggy bank.

Language Arts

Complete the chart.

loud	louder	loudest
short		
kind		

Graphing

Science

Use the graph to answer the questions.

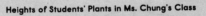

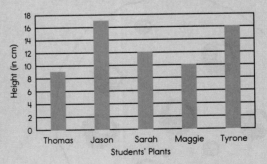

Heights of Students' Plants in Ms. Chung's Class

1. Who has the tallest plant? _____

2. Who has the shortest plant? _____

Extra Credit

Fill in the chart.

Meal	Time of Day
Breakfast	
Snack	
Lunch	
Dinner	

Math

How many fish long is the fishing rod?

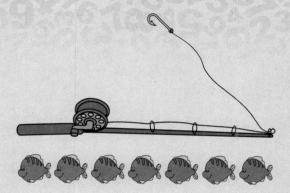

The fishing rod is _____ fish long.

Language Arts

Write the plural for each unit.

1. pound _____

2. gram _____

Measurement

Science

Use the chart to fill in the blanks.

| 100 centimeters = 1 meter |
| 1,000 milligrams = 1 gram |

1. A paper clip has a mass of about 1,000 milligrams, or _____ gram.

2. A baseball bat is about 100 centimeters, or 1 _____ long.

Extra Credit

Who weighs the most in your family? Who weighs the least? How could you find out?

_____

_____

_____

_____

Math

Draw a line to match each number word to its number.

twenty-eight   14

fourteen   5

five   28

Language Arts

Write each number word.

7 _____

8 _____

9 _____

Number Words

Science

Write the number word that tells how many wings a bat has.

_____

Extra Credit

Write the number word that tells how old you are.

_____

Write the number word that tells how many months until your next birthday.

_____

Math

Complete each number sentence.

17 + 30 + 40 = _____

21 + 10 + 11 = _____

8 + 8 + 9 = _____

4 + 5 + 6 = _____

12 + 18 + 21 = _____

Language Arts

Molly ate 4 cherries, 8 grapes, and 1 orange for breakfast. How many pieces of fruit did Molly eat in all?

_____ + _____ + _____ = _____

Fill in the blank with the correct number word.

Molly ate _____ pieces of fruit in all.

Addition

Science

If you poured the 3 beakers of water into 1 larger beaker, how much water would you have?

6 mL
5 mL
4 mL
3 mL
2 mL
1 mL
0 mL

6 mL
5 mL
4 mL
3 mL
2 mL
1 mL
0 mL

6 mL
5 mL
4 mL
3 mL
2 mL
1 mL
0 mL

_____ mL

Extra Credit

What is a strategy that you could use when you add three numbers together?

1 + 3 + 4 = ____

Tell how you would solve this problem.

_____

_____

_____

Math

Write the time shown on the clock.

_____

Language Arts

Ana typed for 7 hours. She typed for 5 more hours later. How many hours did Ana type in all? Use a number word to write the correct answer.

Ana typed for _____ hours in all.

Time

Science

Write a word from the word box to answer each question.

sleep	nocturnal

1. What is an animal that is awake at night?

_____

2. What will that animal probably do during the day?

_____

Extra Credit

Look at a clock and see what time it is. What time will it be in 2 hours?

_____

What time will it be in 12 hours?

_____

Math

Count the objects to help you solve the problem.

_____ – _____ = _____

Language Arts

There are 7 first graders playing on the playground. Three leave to play in the sandbox. How many students are left playing on the playground? Use a number word to write the correct answer.

_____ students are left playing on the playground.

Subtraction

Science

Tyrone's plant measures 10 cm tall. Sarah's plant measures 12 cm tall. How much taller is Sarah's plant? Write a subtraction problem to show how to find the answer.

_____ – _____ = _____

Extra Credit

Write the answers to the facts.

18 – 0 = _____

18 – 1 = _____

18 – 2 = _____

18 – 3 = _____

18 – 4 = _____

18 – 5 = _____

Math

Draw a circle.

Language Arts

Circle the name of the shape that has 6 sides.

A. triangle
B. square
C. hexagon
D. octagon

Shapes

Science

Draw a circle around each item that comes mainly from plants.

Extra Credit

Draw a space creature using only triangles.

Math

Write <, >, or = to make the statement true.

73 ◯ 53

49 ◯ 51

17 ◯ 17

33 ◯ 63

99 ◯ 88

Language Arts

Fill in the blank with the correct answer.

Ten is _____ nineteen.

greater than   less than

Greater Than/ Less Than

Science

Which beaker has less?

_____

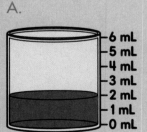

A.

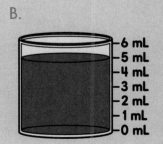

B.

Extra Credit

Write the numbers that are greater than 1 and less than 6.

____

____

____

____

Math

Write the number that is 10 less than the number shown.

39 _____

26 _____

11 _____

101 _____

44 _____

Language Arts

Write the words **tens** and **ones** to show the value of the number.

47 _____

4 _____

7 _____

Place Value

Science

Fill in the chart to show the number values.

Number	Tens	Ones
12	1	2
87		
53		

Extra Credit

How many groups of ten are there in the number **44**?

_____

How many ones are there in the number **32**?

_____

Math

Write the numbers that are missing from the sequence.

17,_____, 19, _____ 21, 22 _____, 24, _____,

_____, _____, 28, _____, 30, _____, _____, 33,

34, _____, 36, _____

Language Arts

Write the name of the insects in order from smallest to largest.

luna moth = 80 mm   flea = 2 mm
bumblebee = 12 mm   grasshopper = 40 mm

_____, _____,

_____, _____

Sequencing Numbers

Science

Number the objects as follows:

1 = long
2 = medium
3 = short

_____   _____   _____

Extra Credit

Fill in the blanks to count backward from 20 to 11.

20   _____

_____   _____

_____   _____

_____   11

Math

Look at the tally chart. How many more children like pepperoni pizza than mushroom pizza?

Favorite Pizza		
Pepperoni	Mushroom	Cheese
IIII	II	III

_____ more children like pepperoni pizza.

Language Arts

Complete the chart with the correct contractions.

can not	can't
do not	
will not	
would not	

Graphing

Science

Use the graph to answer the questions.

1. What day had the most

   rainfall? _____

2. What is the total rainfall for the weekend?

   _____ cm

Rainfall in One Week

Extra Credit

For one week, keep track of the outside temperature each morning at the same time. Then, create a bar graph showing the temperature for each day.

°F	Sun	Mon	Tues	Wed	Thurs	Fri	Sat
100							
90							
80							
70							
60							
50							
40							
30							
20							
10							
0							

Math

How many tennis balls tall is the tennis racket?

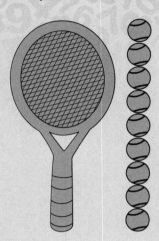

The tennis racket is _____ tennis balls tall.

Language Arts

Write the name of the science tool that would be needed.

clock	ruler	thermometer	scale

1. to measure length _____

2. to measure weight _____

3. to measure temperature _____

4. to measure time

   _____

Measurement

Science

Look at the balance scale.

1. Which is heavier: the apple or the counters?

   _____

2. How do you know? _____

   _____

Extra Credit

How many different ways could a veterinarian measure a dog?

_____

_____

_____

_____

Math

Write the number words to show the value of the number.

30

_____ tens

_____ ones

Language Arts

Write the number word for each.

A. 1 _____

B. 7 _____

C. 8 _____

D. 20 _____

E. 13 _____

Number Words

Science

Write the number word that tells how many legs a spider has.

_____

Extra Credit

Continue the pattern.

twenty-one

twenty-two

_____

_____

_____

twenty-seven

Math

Write the correct answer to each question.

$$\begin{array}{r} 1 \\ +8 \\ \hline \end{array} \qquad \begin{array}{r} 6 \\ +3 \\ \hline \end{array}$$

$$\begin{array}{r} 4 \\ +7 \\ \hline \end{array} \qquad \begin{array}{r} 5 \\ +2 \\ \hline \end{array}$$

$$\begin{array}{r} 3 \\ +9 \\ \hline \end{array} \qquad \begin{array}{r} 8 \\ +6 \\ \hline \end{array}$$

Language Arts

Darron loves trucks. He goes to his dad's job on the weekends. Darron watches the trucks. Sometimes, he can sit on the bulldozer. He likes to watch the trucks move dirt.

Retell the story in your own words. Write at least two sentences.

_____

_____

_____

_____

_____

Addition

Science

1. Circle the sources of water.

2. How many water sources were found in all?

_____

Terra County Landforms			
ponds	2	valleys	1
streams	4	lakes	1

Extra Credit

Fill in the missing addition facts.

$0 + 12 = 12$ \qquad ____ $+ 8 = 12$

____ $+ 11 = 12$ \qquad $5 +$ ____ $= 12$

$2 +$ ____ $= 12$ \qquad ____ $+ 6 + 12$

$3 + 9 = 12$

Math

Draw hands on the clock to show 5:00.

Language Arts

Next to each time, write whether it is day or night.

1. 8:30 p.m. _____

2. 10:00 a.m. _____

3. noon _____

4. midnight _____

5. 3:30 p.m.

   _____

Time

Science

Write **true** or **false**.

1. _____ Earth rotates around on its axis to make day and night.

2. _____ When it is day on one side of Earth, it is night on the other side of Earth.

Extra Credit

Write the months of the year in order from January to December.

_____   _____

_____   _____

_____   _____

_____   _____

_____   _____

_____   _____

Math

Write the correct answer to each problem.

$$
\begin{array}{r} 11 \\ -\ 7 \\ \hline \end{array}
\qquad
\begin{array}{r} 13 \\ -\ 3 \\ \hline \end{array}
$$

$$
\begin{array}{r} 14 \\ -\ 5 \\ \hline \end{array}
\qquad
\begin{array}{r} 9 \\ -\ 0 \\ \hline \end{array}
$$

$$
\begin{array}{r} 15 \\ -\ 8 \\ \hline \end{array}
\qquad
\begin{array}{r} 12 \\ -\ 1 \\ \hline \end{array}
$$

Language Arts

Write the word **true** or **false** on the line.

_____

$5 - 4 = 7 - 6$

Subtraction

Science

Look at the tally chart. How many more people like purple best than like orange best?

Favorite Colors		
Orange	Purple	Green
|||	ⅢⅡ ||	ⅢⅡ	

_____ more people like purple best.

Extra Credit

Fill in the missing subtraction facts.

$15 - 9 = $ _____ $15 - $ _____ $ = 11$

$15 - 8 = 7$ $15 - 3 = $ _____

$15 - 7 = $ _____ $15 - $ _____ $ = 13$

$15 - $ _____ $ = 9$ $15 - 1 = $ _____

$15 - 5 = 10$ $15 - 0 = 15$

Math

Circle the trapezoid.

Language Arts

Write the name of the shape below.

_____

Shapes

Science

Draw a triangle around each item that comes mainly from animals.

Extra Credit

Draw a robot using only circles and rectangles.

Math

Write <, >, or = to make the statement true.

22 $\bigcirc$ 44

36 $\bigcirc$ 35

17 $\bigcirc$ 77

44 $\bigcirc$ 33

81 $\bigcirc$ 18

Language Arts

Fill in the blank with the correct answer.

Thirty is _____ forty.

greater than   less than

Greater Than/ Less Than

Science

Color the beaker that has the greater amount.

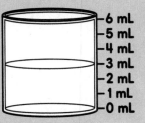 

Extra Credit

Write four numbers that are greater than 20 but less than 30.

_____

_____

_____

_____

Math

Write the number that is 10 more than the number shown.

23 _____

72 _____

91 _____

2 _____

Language Arts

Write the words **tens** and **ones** to show the value of the number.

28

2 _____

8 _____

Place Value

Science

Fill in the chart to show the number values.

Number	Tens	Ones
29	2	9
97		
34		

Extra Credit

How many ones are there in the number **67**?

_____

How many groups of ten are there in the number **11**?

_____

Math

Write the numbers that are missing from the sequence.

70, _____, 72, _____, 74, _____, _____, 77,

_____, 79, _____, _____, _____, 83, _____,

_____, _____, 87

Language Arts

Write the missing number words.

one, _____, three, _____, _____, 6

Sequencing Numbers

Science

Write the numbers 1 to 4 to order the students from shortest to tallest.

_____ Sofia 97 cm

_____ Parker 121 cm

_____ Lily 119 cm

_____ Nathan 108 cm

Extra Credit

Fill in the blanks to count by tens to 100.

10   _____

_____   _____

_____   _____

_____   100

Math

Look at the tally chart. How many more medium-sized dogs than large dogs live on Hay Street?

Dogs on Hay Street		
Small	Medium	Large
ΗΗΙΙΙ	ΗΗΙΙ	ΙΙΙ

_____ more medium-sized dogs than large dogs live on Hay Street.

Language Arts

Complete the chart with the correct contractions.

I had	I'd
she had	
he had	
we had	

Graphing

Science

Complete the chart.
1. Look around your classroom. List items you think are magnetic and items you think are not magnetic.

Magnetic	Not Magnetic

2. What is the same about the items in the magnetic column? _____

_____

Extra Credit

Use the chart to color the bar graph.

Magnet Shape	Number of Paper Clips It Held
bar	5
horseshoe	7
ring	3

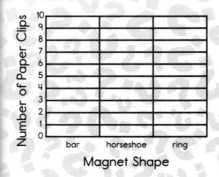

Magnet Shape

Math

How many fish tall is the fisherman?

The fisherman is _____ fish tall.

Language Arts

A baby rabbit is 5 inches long. Its mother is 12 inches long. How many inches longer is the mother rabbit? Use a number word to write the correct answer.

_____

Write the abbreviation for **inches**.

_____

Measurement

Science

Fill in the blanks with the correct unit of measure.

centimeters	grams	seconds

A. A banana has a mass of about 140 _____.

B. It takes about 15 _____ to say the alphabet.

C. A pencil is about 17 _____ long.

Extra Credit

Measure three things in your room. Write the names of the objects in order from largest to smallest.

1. _____

2. _____

3. _____

Math

Write the number words to show the value of the number.

27

_____ tens

_____ ones

Language Arts

Write the number word for each.

A. 11 _____

B. 3 _____

C. 5 _____

D. 9 _____

E. 18 _____

Number Words

Science

Write the number word that tells how many legs an ant has.

_____

Extra Credit

Continue the pattern.

fifty-one

fifty-two

_____

_____

_____

_____

fifty-seven

fifty-eight

_____

Math

Write the correct answer to each question.

```
  6        1
  1        2
+ 9      + 4
```

```
  5        9
  7        4
+ 3      + 6
```

Language Arts

Mrs. Avery bought 5 boxes of pasta, 3 bananas, and 9 muffins at the grocery store. How many food items did Mrs. Avery buy in all?

_____ + _____ + _____ = _____

Write the answer as a number word.

_____

Addition

Science

At breakfast, Maddie observed the animals in her yard. She saw 3 squirrels. Each grabbed 1 acorn to eat. A bird also ate 1 acorn. Then, 2 more squirrels each ate 1 acorn.

How many acorns did Maddie see animals eat?

_____

Extra Credit

Fill in the missing addition facts.

$0 + 13 = 13$ $4 + \underline{\quad} = 13$

$1 + \underline{\quad} = 13$ $\underline{\quad} + 8 = 13$

$\underline{\quad} + 11 = 13$ $6 + 7 = \underline{\quad}$

$3 + 10 = 13$

Math

Write the time shown on the clock.

10:00

Language Arts

In a complete sentence, tell an activity you do in each season.

1. spring vakks
2. summer Scummer
3. autumn we Baskball
4. winter Hrowesnow

Science

Circle the correct answer.

If it is 11:00 pm, what time is it a half hour later?

A. 12:00 p.m.
B. 11:30 p.m.
C. 11:30 a.m.
D. 12:00 a.m.

Time

Extra Credit

What is your favorite season? Why? Draw a picture of your favorite activity for that season.

Summer and spring

Math

Write the correct answer to each problem.

$$
\begin{array}{r} 9 \\ -5 \\ \hline 4 \end{array}
\qquad
\begin{array}{r} 6 \\ -4 \\ \hline 2 \end{array}
$$

$$
\begin{array}{r} 12 \\ -2 \\ \hline 10 \end{array}
\qquad
\begin{array}{r} 8 \\ -5 \\ \hline 3 \end{array}
$$

$$
\begin{array}{r} 14 \\ -6 \\ \hline \end{array}
\qquad
\begin{array}{r} 7 \\ -2 \\ \hline 5 \end{array}
$$

Language Arts

Seventeen fish are in the coral. Eight swim away. How many fish are left in the coral? Use a number word to write the correct answer.

____9____ fish are left in the coral.

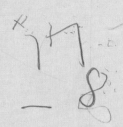

Subtraction

Science

The ball bounced 50 cm on the classroom floor. It only bounced 30 cm on the carpet.

How much higher did the ball bounce on the classroom floor than on the carpet?

_____ cm

Write a number sentence to show how to find the answer.

_____ − _____ = _____

Extra Credit

Fill in the missing subtraction facts.

13 − 10 = 3   13 − ____ = 9

13 − 9 = 4   13 − 3 = 10

13 − 8 = 5   13 − 2 = ____

13 − 7 = 6   13 − 1 = 12

13 − 6 = ____   13 − 0 = ____

13 − ____ = 8

Math

Draw a rectangle.

Language Arts

Write a sentence that describes a square.

_____

_____

_____

Shapes

Science

Draw a rectangle around each tool that could help you observe how quickly the moon travels across the sky.

magnifying glass   telescope   compass

pencil   camera   notebook

Extra Credit

Cut out a variety of shapes from colored construction paper. Then, glue the shapes onto a large sheet of paper to make a shape collage.

Math

Write <, >, or = to make the statement true.

14 ◯ 32

41 ◯ 40

11 ◯ 22

66 ◯ 64

39 ◯ 28

Language Arts

Fill in the blank with the correct answer.

Sixty is_____ twenty.

greater than   less than

Greater Than/ Less Than

Science

Color the picture that is less than 4 paper clips long.

Extra Credit

Write a number that is greater than 90, but less than 100.

_____

Write a number that is greater than 18, but less than 23.

_____

Math

Write the value of the number.

80

_____ tens

_____ ones

Language Arts

Write the words **tens** and **ones** to show the value of the number.

94

9 _____

4 _____

Place Value

Science

Fill in the chart to show the number values.

Number	Tens	Ones
19	1	9
48		
72		

Extra Credit

How many groups of ten are there in the number **36**?

_____

How many ones are there in the number **46**?

_____

Math

Write the numbers that are missing from the sequence.

10, _____, 30, 40, 50, _____, 70, _____, 90,

_____, _____, 120, _____, 140, _____

Language Arts

Write the missing number words.

fifteen, _____, seventeen,

_____, _____,

_____, twenty-one

Sequencing Numbers

Science

Amy and John conducted an experiment to see which of their magnets was the strongest. Use their chart to answer the questions.

Magent Shape	Number of Paper Clips It Held
bar	5
horseshoe	7
ring	3
rectangle	6
sphere	2

Which magnet held the most paper clips?

_____

Extra Credit

Fill in the blanks to count by twos from 0 to 20.

0

_____

_____

_____

_____

_____

_____

_____

_____

20

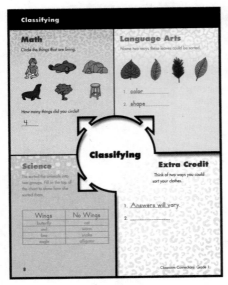

Page 8

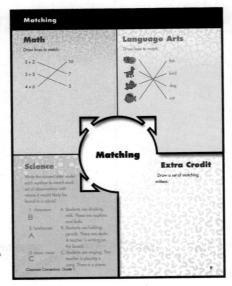

Page 9

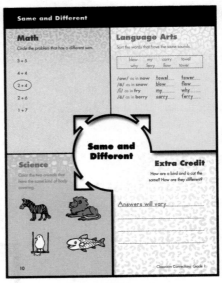

Page 10

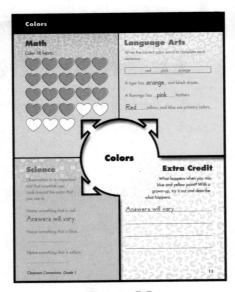

Page 11

Page 12

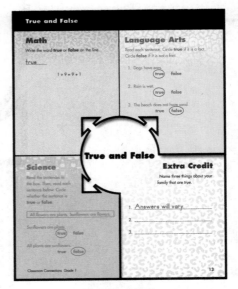

Page 13

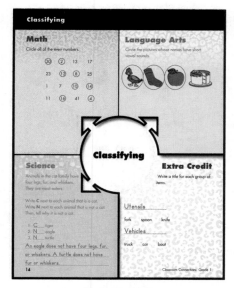

Page 14

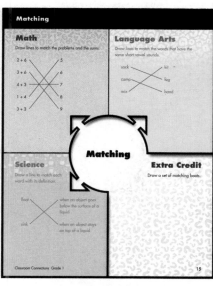

Page 15

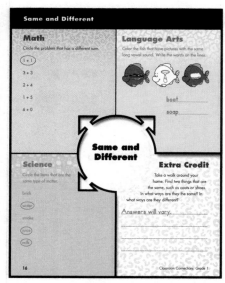

Page 16

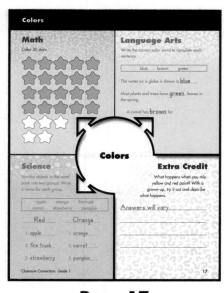

Page 17

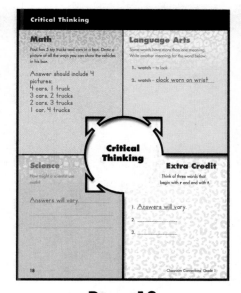

Page 18

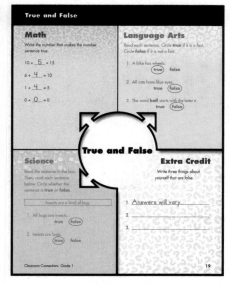

Page 19

Page 20

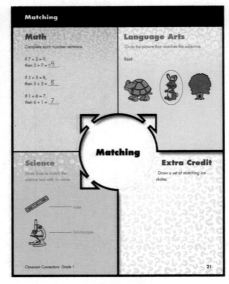

Page 21

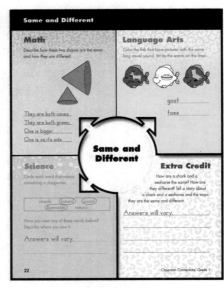

Page 22

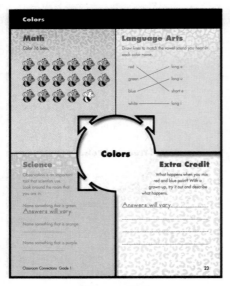

Page 23

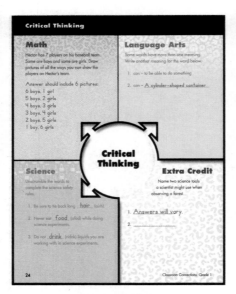

Page 24

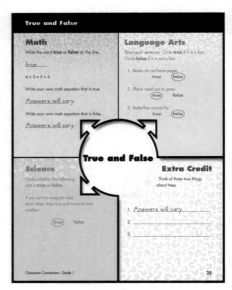

Page 25

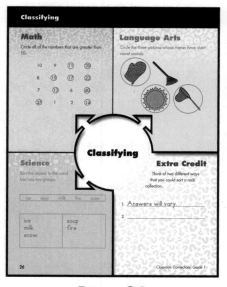

Page 26

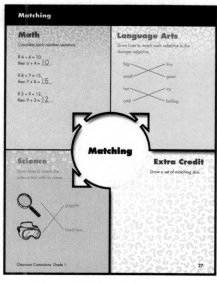

Page 27

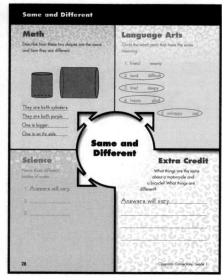

Page 28

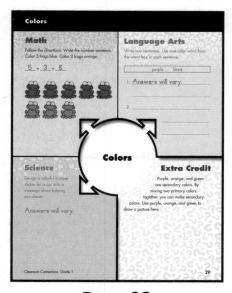

Page 29

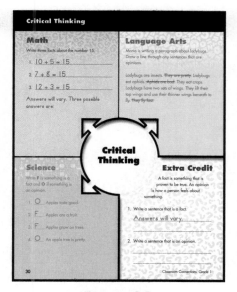

Page 30

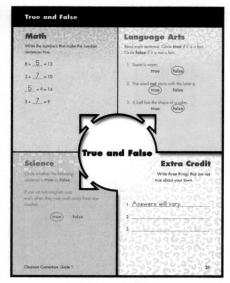

Page 31

Classroom Connections Grade 1

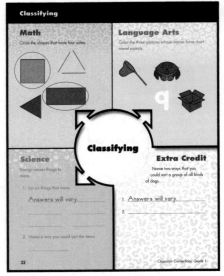

Page 32

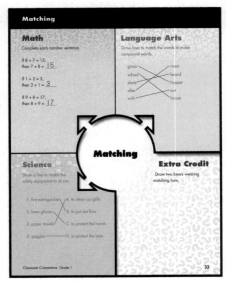

Page 33

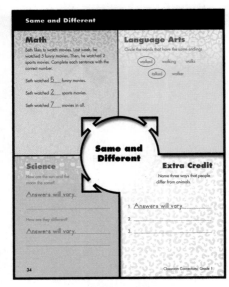

Page 34

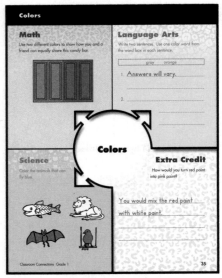

Page 35

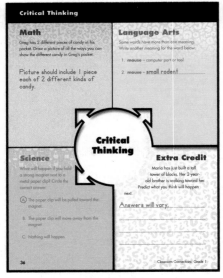

Page 36

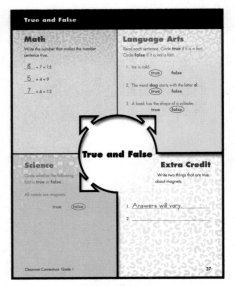

Page 37

Page 38

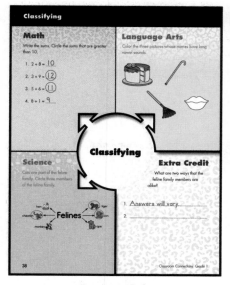

Classifying

Math
Write the sums. Circle the sums that are greater than 10.

1. $2 + 8 = $ 10
2. $3 + 9 = $ (12)
3. $5 + 6 = $ (11)
4. $8 + 1 = $ 9

Language Arts
Color the three pictures whose names have long vowel sounds.

Science
Cats are part of the feline family. Circle three members of the feline family.

Felines

Classifying

Extra Credit
What are two ways that the feline family members are alike?

1. Answers will vary.
2.

Page 38

Page 39

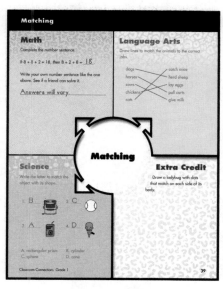

Matching

Math
Complete the number sentence.

If $8 + 8 + 2 = 18$, then $8 + 2 + 8 = $ 18

Write your own number sentence like the one above. See if a friend can solve it.

Answers will vary.

Language Arts
Draw lines to match the animals to the correct jobs.

dogs — catch mice
horses — herd sheep
cows — lay eggs
chickens — pull carts
cats — give milk

Science
Write the letter to match the object with its shape.

1. B
2. C
3. A
4. D

A. rectangular prism   B. cylinder
C. sphere   D. cone

Matching

Extra Credit
Draw a ladybug with dots that match on each side of its body.

Page 39

Page 40

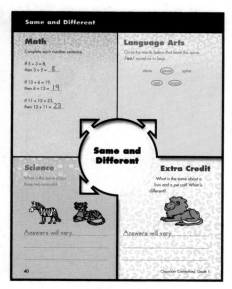

Same and Different

Math
Complete each number sentence.

If $5 + 3 = 8$, then $3 + 5 = $ 8

If $13 + 6 = 19$, then $6 + 13 = $ 19

If $11 + 12 = 23$, then $12 + 11 = $ 23

Language Arts
Circle the words below that have the same /oo/ sound as in loop.

stone   (spoon)   spine
(pool)   (moon)

Science
What is the same about these two animals?

Answers will vary.

Same and Different

Extra Credit
What is the same about a lion and a pet cat? What is different?

Answers will vary.

Page 40

Page 41

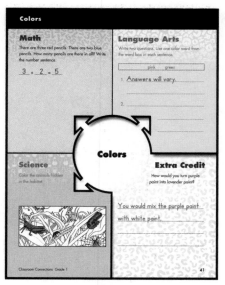

Colors

Math
There are three red pencils. There are two blue pencils. How many pencils are there in all? Write the number sentence.

$3 + 2 = 5$

Language Arts
Write two questions. Use one color word from the word box in each sentence.

pink   green

1. Answers will vary.

2.

Science
Color the animals hidden in the habitat.

Colors

Extra Credit
How would you turn purple paint into lavender paint?

You would mix the purple paint with white paint.

Page 41

Page 42

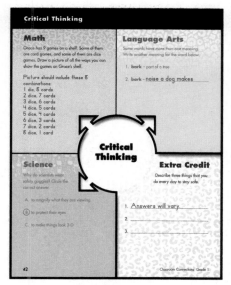

Critical Thinking

Math
Grace has 9 games on a shelf. Some of them are card games, and some of them are dice games. Draw a picture of all the ways you can show the games on Grace's shelf.

Picture should include these 8 combinations:
1 die, 8 cards
2 dice, 7 cards
3 dice, 6 cards
4 dice, 5 cards
5 dice, 4 cards
6 dice, 3 cards
7 dice, 2 cards
8 dice, 1 card

Language Arts
Some words have more than one meaning. Write another meaning for the word below.

1. bark – part of a tree

2. bark - noise a dog makes

Science
Why do scientists wear safety goggles? Circle the correct answer.

A. to magnify what they are viewing

B. to protect their eyes

C. to make things look 3-D

Critical Thinking

Extra Credit
Describe three things that you do every day to stay safe.

1. Answers will vary.
2.
3.

Page 42

Page 43

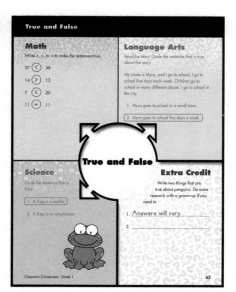

True and False

Math
Write <, >, or = to make the statement true.

27 (<) 38
14 (>) 13
7 (<) 20
11 (=) 11

Language Arts
Read the story. Circle the sentence that is true about the story.

My name is Myra, and I go to school. I go to school five days each week. Children go to school in many different places. I go to school in the city.

1. Myra goes to school in a small town.

2. Myra goes to school five days a week.

Science
Circle the sentence that is false.

1. A frog is a reptile.

2. A frog is an amphibian.

True and False

Extra Credit
Write two things that are true about penguins. Do some research with a grown-up if you need to.

1. Answers will vary.
2.

Page 43

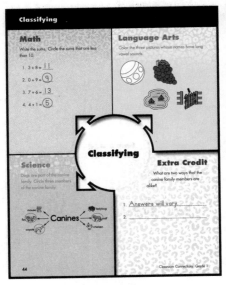

Page 44

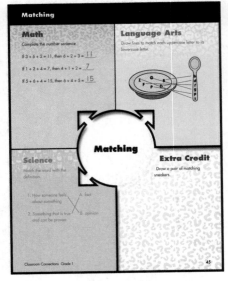

Page 45

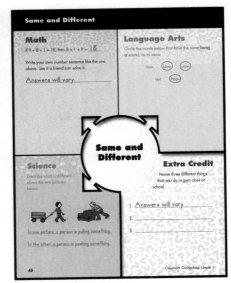

Page 46

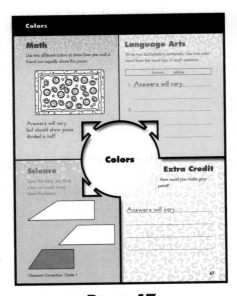

Page 47

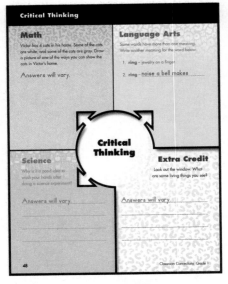

Page 48

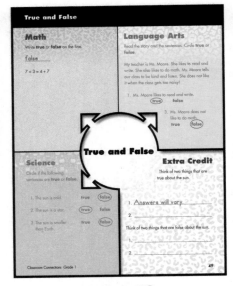

Page 49

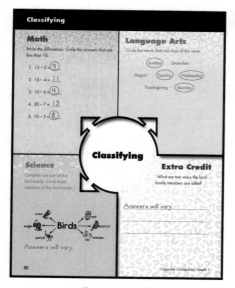

Page 50

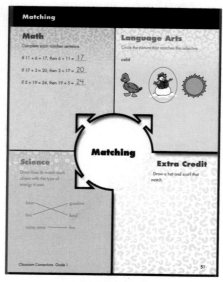

Page 51

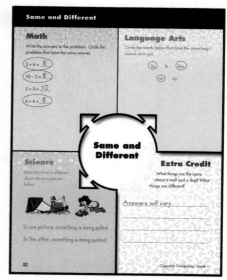

Page 52

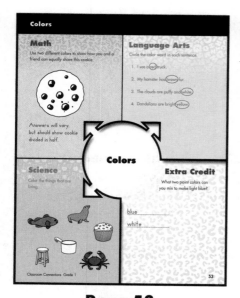

Page 53

Page 54

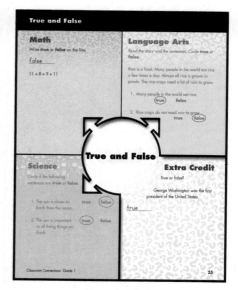

Page 55

Page 56

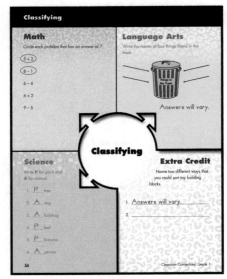

Classifying

Math
Circle each problem that has an answer of 7.
- (5 + 2)
- (8 - 1)
- 6 - 4
- 6 + 2
- 9 - 5

Language Arts
Write the names of four things found in the trash.

Answers will vary.

Science
Write **P** for plant and **A** for animal.
1. P tree
2. A dog
3. A ladybug
4. P leaf
5. P banana
6. A person

Extra Credit
Name two different ways that you could sort toy building blocks.
1. Answers will vary.
2.

Page 56

Page 57

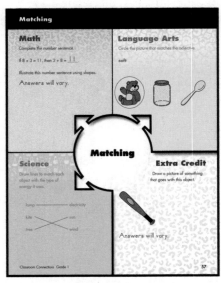

Matching

Math
Complete the number sentence.
If 8 + 3 = 11, then 3 + 8 = 11

Illustrate this number sentence using shapes.
Answers will vary.

Language Arts
Circle the picture that matches the adjective.
soft

Science
Draw lines to match each object with the type of energy it uses.
jump — electricity
kite — sun
tree — wind

Extra Credit
Draw a picture of something that goes with this object.

Answers will vary.

Page 57

Page 58

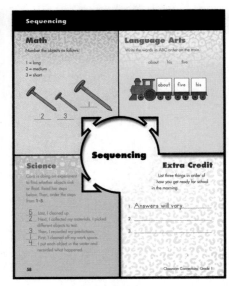

Sequencing

Math
Number the objects as follows:
1 = long
2 = medium
3 = short

Language Arts
Write the words in ABC order on the train.
about   his   five

about | five | his

Science
Cara is doing an experiment to find whether objects sink or float. Read her steps below. Then, order the steps from 1–5.
5 Last, I cleaned up.
2 Next, I collected my materials. I picked different objects to test.
3 Then, I recorded my predictions.
1 First, I cleaned off my work space.
4 I put each object in the water and recorded what happened.

Extra Credit
List three things in order of how you get ready for school in the morning.
1. Answers will vary.
2.
3.

Page 58

Page 59

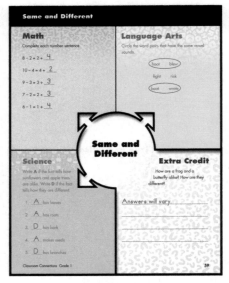

Same and Different

Math
Complete each number sentence.
8 - 2 = 2 + 4
10 - 4 = 4 + 2
9 - 3 = 3 + 3
7 - 2 = 2 + 3
6 - 1 = 1 + 4

Language Arts
Circle the word pairs that have the same vowel sounds.
(hoot   blew)
fight   risk
(boat   wrote)

Science
Write **A** if the fact tells how sunflowers and apple trees are alike. Write **D** if the fact tells how they are different.
1. A has leaves
2. A has roots
3. D has bark
4. A makes seeds
5. D has branches

Extra Credit
How are a frog and a butterfly alike? How are they different?

Answers will vary.

Page 59

Page 60

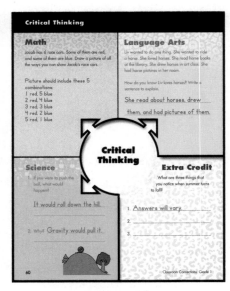

Critical Thinking

Math
Jacob has 6 race cars. Some of them are red, and some of them are blue. Draw a picture of all the ways you can show Jacob's race cars.

Picture should include these 5 combinations:
1 red, 5 blue
2 red, 4 blue
3 red, 3 blue
4 red, 2 blue
5 red, 1 blue

Language Arts
Liv wanted to do one thing. She wanted to ride a horse. She loved horses. She read horse books at the library. She drew horses in art class. She had horse pictures in her room.

How do you know Liv loves horses? Write a sentence to explain.

She read about horses, drew them, and had pictures of them.

Science
1. If you were to push the ball, what would happen?
It would roll down the hill.

2. Why? Gravity would pull it.

Extra Credit
What are three things that you notice when summer turns to fall?
1. Answers will vary.
2.
3.

Page 60

Page 61

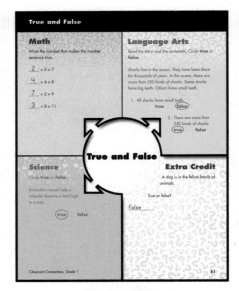

True and False

Math
Write the number that makes the number sentence true.
2 + 5 = 7
4 + 4 = 8
7 + 2 = 9
3 + 8 = 11

Language Arts
Read the story and the sentences. Circle **true** or **false**.

Sharks live in the ocean. They have been there for thousands of years. In the ocean, there are more than 350 kinds of sharks. Some sharks have big teeth. Others have small teeth.

1. All sharks have small teeth.
   true   (false)

2. There are more than 350 kinds of sharks.
   (true)   false

Science
Circle **true** or **false**.

A dog is in the feline family of animals.
True or false?
false

Binoculars would help a scientist observe a bird high in a tree.
(true)   false

Extra Credit

Page 61

230

Classroom Connections Grade 1

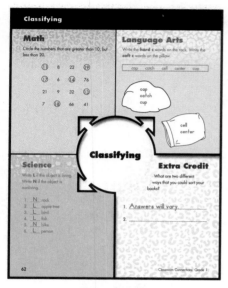

Page 62

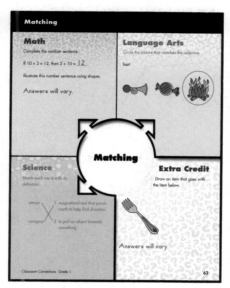

Page 63

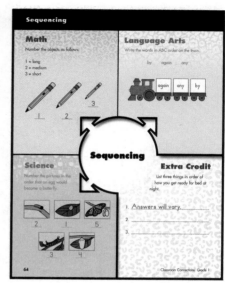

Page 64

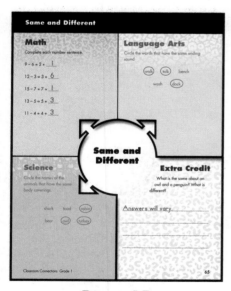

Page 65

Page 66

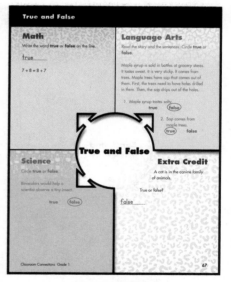

Page 67

Answer Key

Page 68

Classifying

Math
Circle all of the even numbers.

11 (10) 9 29

(14) 7 15 17

3 (22) (16) 27

(4) 13 15 35

Language Arts
Write the **hard g** words on the rock. Write the **soft g** words on the pillow.

germ get giraffe Gus gust

get
Gus
gust

germ
giraffe

Classifying

Science
What makes something living? Discuss your answer with a friend.

Answers will vary.

Extra Credit
Think of two ways that you could sort your favorite collection.

1. Answers will vary.
2.

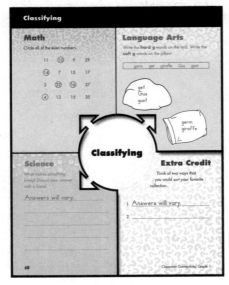

Page 69

Sequencing

Math
Number the objects as follows:

1 = long
2 = medium
3 = short

3 2 1

Language Arts
Write the missing days of the week in the correct order.

Saturday Monday Wednesday

Sunday, Monday, Tuesday, Wednesday,
Thursday, Friday, Saturday.

Sequencing

Science
Put the following bodies of water in order from smallest to largest.

lake ocean pond puddle

puddle
pond
lake
ocean

Extra Credit
Write a story about a time that you were proud. Make sure the story has a beginning, a middle, and an end.

Answers will vary.

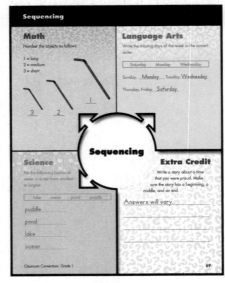

Page 70

Matching

Math
Complete each number sentence.

$7 - 4 = 2 + 1$
$12 - 8 = 1 + 3$
$16 - 4 = 4 + 8$
$11 - 1 = 3 + 7$
$15 - 2 = 2 + 11$

Language Arts
A prefix is a part of a word. It is at the beginning.

Draw a line to match each prefix to the correct meaning.

dis——————before
un——————not
re-——————not
pre-——————again

Matching

Science
Match each word with its definition.

magnet — 1. an object that attracts materials made of iron or steel

repel — 2. to push an object away from something

Extra Credit
Draw an item that goes with the item below.

Answers will vary.

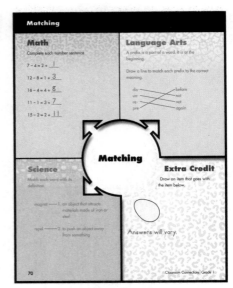

Page 71

Same and Different

Math
Kennedy collects bugs. She collected 13 ladybugs in one jar. She collected 5 lightning bugs in another jar. Complete each sentence with the correct number.

Kennedy collected 13 ladybugs.
Kennedy collected 5 lightning bugs.
Kennedy collected 18 bugs in all.

Language Arts
Circle the word pairs that sound the same.

one won
big bag
two too

Same and Different

Science
Name three different things that plants need to grow.

1. Answers will vary.
2.
3.

Extra Credit
What is the same about a shark and a goldfish? What is different?

Answers will vary.

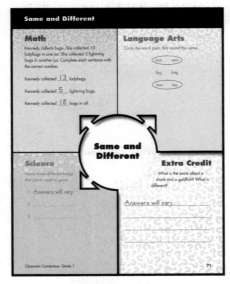

Page 72

Sequencing

Math
Number the items as follows:

1 = long
2 = medium
3 = short

3 2 1

Language Arts
Write the bug names in ABC order.

grasshopper ant ladybug
caterpillar centipede

1. ant
2. caterpillar
3. centipede
4. grasshopper
5. ladybug

Sequencing

Science
Use the word bank to label the pictures of the life cycle of a pumpkin.

flower orange pumpkin seed vine

seed sprout vine
flower green pumpkin orange pumpkin

Extra Credit
Retell the story of Cinderella to a friend. What happens first? What happens next? What happens at the end?

Answers will vary.

Page 73

Critical Thinking

Math
Sarah has 7 toy horses. Some of them are brown, and some of them are gray. Draw a picture of all the ways you can show Sarah's horses.
Picture should include these 6 combinations:
1 brown, 6 gray
2 brown, 5 gray
3 brown, 4 gray
4 brown, 3 gray
5 brown, 2 gray
6 brown, 1 gray

Language Arts
Josie is getting ready for bed. She is tired. She puts on her pajamas. Her cat Paws is under the bed. He leaps out and jumps on Josie's pant leg. Josie screams! Paws surprises her. Then, Josie sees Paws run out of her room.

Why do you think Paws ran? Write a sentence.

Answers will vary.

Critical Thinking

Science
Circle the best answer.

Which would be better to use to collect water?

bucket net goggles

Extra Credit
What science tool would you use to look closely at a flower petal?

hand lens

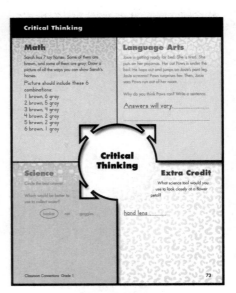

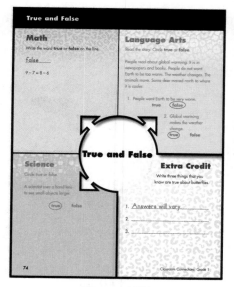

Page 74

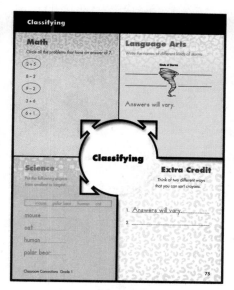

Page 75

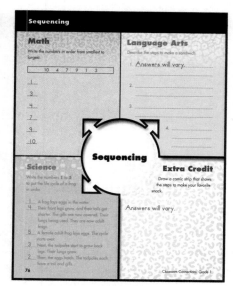

Page 76

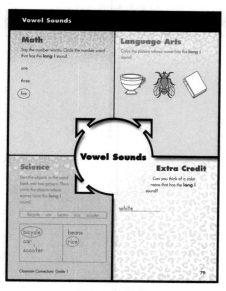

Page 79

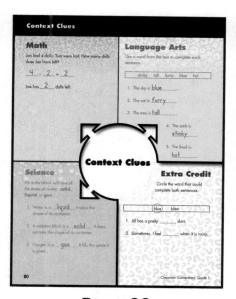

Page 80

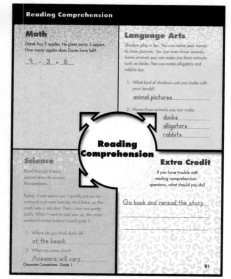

Page 81

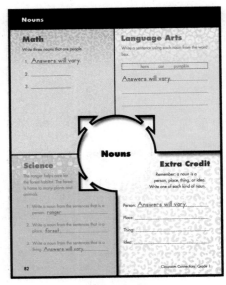

Nouns

Math
Write three nouns that are people.
1. Answers will vary.
2. _____
3. _____

Language Arts
Write a sentence using each noun from the word box.

horn   car   pumpkin

Answers will vary.
_____
_____

Nouns

Science
The ranger helps care for the forest habitat. The forest is home to many plants and animals.
1. Write a noun from the sentences that is a person. ranger
2. Write a noun from the sentences that is a place. forest
3. Write a noun from the sentences that is a thing. Answers will vary.

Extra Credit
Remember: a noun is a person, place, thing, or idea. Write one of each kind of noun.
Person: Answers will vary.
Place: _____
Thing: _____
Idea: _____

82

Page 82

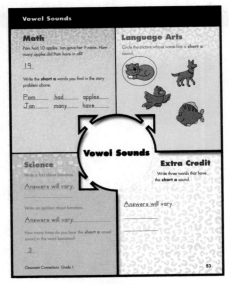

Vowel Sounds

Math
Pam had 10 apples. Jan gave her 9 more. How many apples did Pam have in all?
19
Write the **short a** words you find in the story problem above.
Pam   had   apples
Jan   many   have

Language Arts
Circle the picture whose name has a **short a** sound.

Vowel Sounds

Science
Write a fact about bananas.
Answers will vary.

Write an opinion about bananas.
Answers will vary.

How many times do you hear the **short a** vowel sound in the word bananas?
3

Extra Credit
Write three words that have the **short a** sound.
Answers will vary.

Classroom Connections Grade 1

83

Page 83

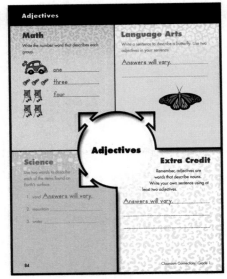

Adjectives

Math
Write the number word that describes each group.
one
three
four

Language Arts
Write a sentence to describe a butterfly. Use two adjectives in your sentence.
Answers will vary.

Adjectives

Science
Use two words to describe each of the items found on Earth's surface.
1. sand Answers will vary.
2. mountain
3. water

Extra Credit
Remember, adjectives are words that describe nouns. Write your own sentence using at least two adjectives.
Answers will vary.

84

Classroom Connections Grade 1

Page 84

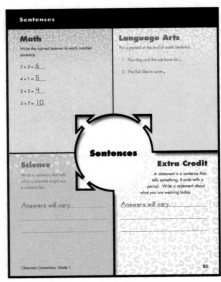

Sentences

Math
Write the correct answer to each number sentence.
$3 + 3 = 6$
$4 + 1 = 5$
$2 + 2 = 4$
$3 + 7 = 10$

Language Arts
Put a period at the end of each sentence.
1. The dog and the cat here for .
2. The fish like to swim .

Sentences

Science
Write a sentence that tells what a scientist might use a camera for.
Answers will vary.

Extra Credit
A statement is a sentence that tells something. It ends with a period. Write a statement about what you are wearing today.
Answers will vary.

Classroom Connections Grade 1

85

Page 85

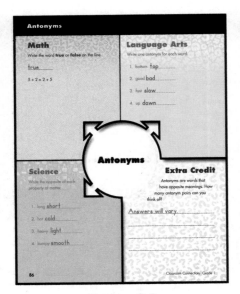

Antonyms

Math
Write the word **true** or **false** on the line.
true
$5 + 2 = 2 + 5$

Language Arts
Write one antonym for each word.
1. bottom top
2. good bad
3. fast slow
4. up down

Antonyms

Science
Write the opposite of each property of matter.
1. long short
2. hot cold
3. heavy light
4. bumpy smooth

Extra Credit
Antonyms are words that have opposite meanings. How many antonym pairs can you think of?
Answers will vary.

86

Classroom Connections Grade 1

Page 86

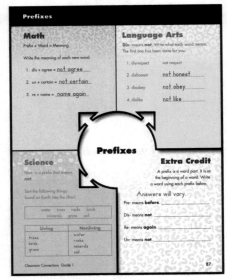

Prefixes

Math
Prefix + Word = Meaning
Write the meaning of each new word.
1. dis + agree = not agree
2. un + certain = not certain
3. re + name = name again

Language Arts
Dis- means **not**. Write what each word means. The first one has been done for you.
1. disrespect not respect
2. dishonest not honest
3. disobey not obey
4. dislike not like

Prefixes

Science
Non- is a prefix that means not.
Sort the following things found on Earth into the chart.

water   trees   rocks   birds
minerals   grass   soil

Living	Nonliving
trees	water
birds	rocks
grass	minerals
	soil

Extra Credit
A prefix is a word part. It is at the beginning of a word. Write a word using each prefix below.
Answers will vary.
Pre- means **before**. _____
Dis- means **not**. _____
Re- means **again**. _____
Un- means **not**. _____

Classroom Connections Grade 1

87

Page 87

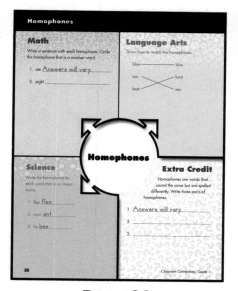

Page 88

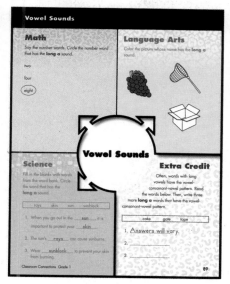

Page 89

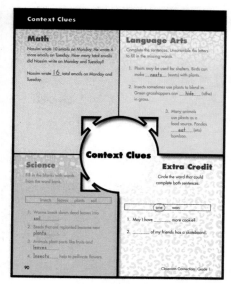

Page 90

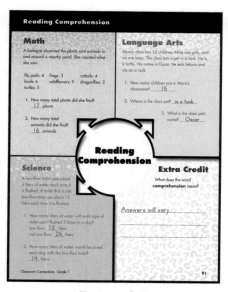

Page 91

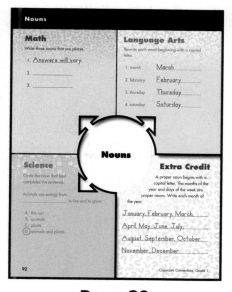

Page 92

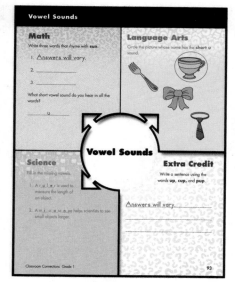

Page 93

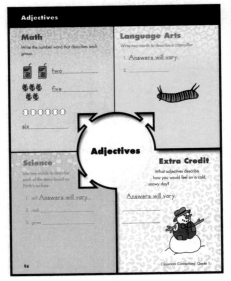

Page 94

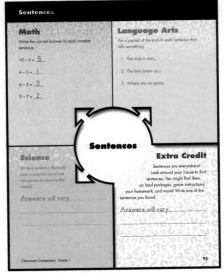

Page 95

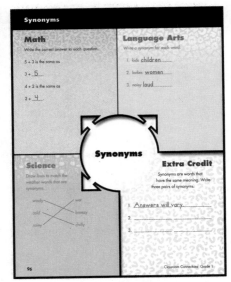

Page 96

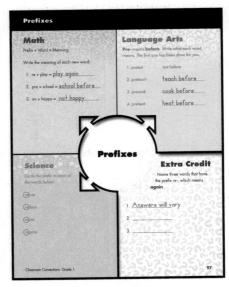

Page 97

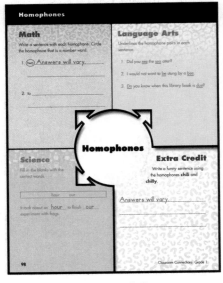

Page 98

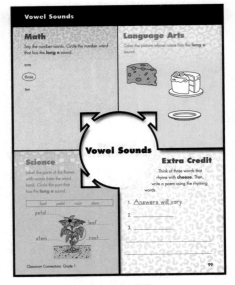

Page 99

Classroom Connections Grade 1

Page 100

Reading Comprehension

Math
Maggie picks 6 flowers. Her mom gives her 2 more flowers. How many flowers does Maggie have?

Maggie has __8__ flowers.

Language Arts
Read the story and answer the questions.

Lila's school is on a busy street in the city. A fence is around the outside of the school. There is a basketball hoop and court. There is also a playground with a slide.

1. Where is Lila's school?
on a busy street in the city

2. List three things at Lila's school.
Answers will vary.

Science
Olivia and Mason each built a bridge with toothpicks. They then tested which bridge was stronger by placing coins on top. Olivia's bridge held 29 pennies before it began to break. Mason's bridge held 24 nickels before it began to break.

1. What makes it hard to tell whose bridge was stronger?
The bridges were tested with different types of coins.

Extra Credit
Tell what happens in your favorite part of your favorite book.
Answers will vary.

Page 101

Suffixes

Math
Add the suffix -er to each word. Then, write the word.

1. call + er = caller
2. farm + er = farmer
3. dream + er = dreamer
4. sing + er = singer

Language Arts
Write what each word means. The first one has been done for you.

1. painter — one who paints
2. seller — one who sells
3. bowler — one who bowls
4. driver — one who drives

Science
Find and circle the suffix -er in each sentence below.

The speaker talked about how to grow vegetables.
She is an expert gardener.
Every listener was fascinated by her stories.

Extra Credit
A suffix is a word part. It is at the end of a word. Write a word using each suffix below.
Answers will vary.
-er means one who
-ful means full of
-less means without
-ly means in a certain way

Page 102

Nouns

Math
Write three nouns that are things.

1. Answers will vary.
2.
3.

Language Arts
A noun is a person, place, thing, or idea. Write one noun to fit each of these categories.

1. person: Answers will vary.
2. place:
3. thing:
4. idea:

Science
Circle the noun that best completes the sentence.
Plants get energy from _____ to live and to grow.
A. animals
B. the sun
C. wind
D. other plants

Extra Credit
Examples of nouns that are ideas are **freedom**, **happiness**, and **friendship**. Can you think of more nouns that are ideas?
Answers will vary.

Page 103

Context Clues

Math
Five lights were on in the house. James turned off 3 lights. How many lights are still on in the house?

5 - 3 = 2

There are __2__ lights still on in the house.

Language Arts
A conjunction joins two words, phrases, or sentences. Use the words in the box to complete the sentences.

and   but   so

1. Casey found a penny _and_ put it in her pocket.
2. Hector wanted to wear shorts, _but_ it was snowing.
3. Julia will go to bed now, _so_ it is time to turn off her light.

Science
Fill in the blanks with words from the word box.

bones   heart   lungs   muscles

1. Your _bones_ give your body its structure.
2. You use your _muscles_ to move body parts.
3. Your _lungs_ are used to breathe.
4. Your _heart_ pumps blood through your body.

Extra Credit
Circle the word that could complete both sentences.

grate   (great)

1. I had a _____ time at the party.
2. Katie is a _____ friend.

Page 104

Adjectives

Math
Write the number word that describes each group.

eight
seven

Language Arts
Write a sentence to describe a teddy bear. Use two adjectives in your sentence.
Answers will vary.

Science
Think of your sense of taste and answer the questions below.

1. What is your favorite food?
Answers will vary.

2. Is it bitter, salty, sweet, or sour?

Extra Credit
What adjectives describe how you would feel on a hot, sunny day?
Answers will vary.

Page 105

Sentences

Math
Write 12 question marks on the lines below.

? ? ? ?
? ? ? ?
? ? ? ?

Language Arts
Write a question mark at the end of each asking sentence.

1. Will we bake a cake ?
2. Do we have eggs ?
3. Shall we use chocolate frosting ?

Science
Scientists ask many questions. Fill in the blanks with letters to complete the question words.

1. w h o
2. w h a t
3. w h e r e
4. w h e n

Extra Credit
Question words are important. They help you find information. Use each word to write a question.

Who or What? Answers will vary.
Where?
When?
Why?
How?

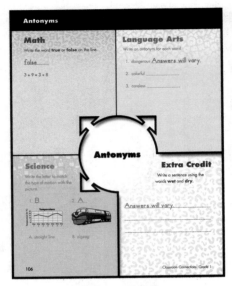

Page 106

Antonyms

Math
Write the word **true** or **false** on the line.

false

$3 + 9 = 3 + 8$

Language Arts
Write an antonym for each word.

1. dangerous Answers will vary.

2. colorful _____

3. careless _____

Antonyms

Science
Write the letter to match the type of motion with the picture.

1. B   2. A

A. straight line   B. zigzag

Extra Credit
Write a sentence using the words **wet** and **dry**.

Answers will vary. _____

106   Classroom Connections Grade 1

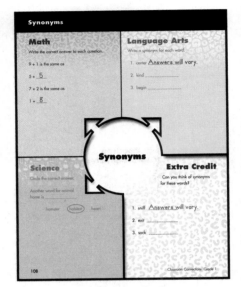

Page 107

Verbs

Math
This is a verb web. Write six verbs on the lines.

(Verbs)

Answers will vary.

Language Arts
Circle each verb.

1. Yosef rides his bike.

2. Claire holds the fork.

3. Mia smells the food.

4. Taylor sees her mom.

Verbs

Science
Use a verb, or action word, to tell how each animal moves.

1. snake Answers will vary.

2. bird

3. kangaroo

4. cheetah

Extra Credit
Some verbs are action words. They show movement. Write three action verbs.

1. Answers will vary.

2. _____

3. _____

Classroom Connections Grade 1   107

Page 108

Synonyms

Math
Write the correct answer to each question.

9 + 1 is the same as

5 + 5

7 + 2 is the same as

1 + 8

Language Arts
Write a synonym for each word.

1. center Answers will vary.

2. kind _____

3. begin _____

Synonyms

Science
Circle the correct answer.

Another word for animal home is

hamster   (habitat)   heart

Extra Credit
Can you think of synonyms for these words?

1. sniff Answers will vary.

2. exit _____

3. sack _____

108   Classroom Connections Grade 1

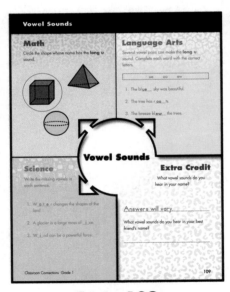

Page 109

Vowel Sounds

Math
Circle the shape whose name has the **long u** sound.

Language Arts
Several vowel pairs can make the **long u** sound. Complete each word with the correct letters.

ue   oo   ew

1. The bl ue _ sky is beautiful.

2. The tree has r oo _ ts.

3. The breeze bl ew _ the trees.

Vowel Sounds

Science
Write the missing vowels in each sentence.

1. W a t e r changes the shapes of the land.

2. A glacier is a large mass of i ce.

3. W i nd can be a powerful force.

Extra Credit
What vowel sounds do you hear in your name?

Answers will vary. _____

What vowel sounds do you hear in your best friend's name?

Classroom Connections Grade 1   109

Page 110

Homophones

Math
Write a sentence with each homophone. Circle the homophone that is a number word.

1. (one) Answers will vary.

2. won _____

Language Arts
Draw lines to match the homophones.

aunt — flour
flower — deer
deer — ant

Homophones

Science
Write a homophone for each word. Circle the homophone in each pair that is an animal name.

1. (hare) hair

2. bare (bear)

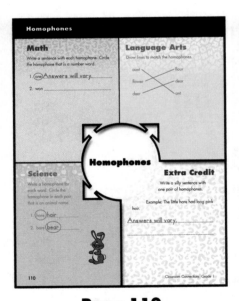

Extra Credit
Write a silly sentence with one pair of homophones.

Example: The little hare had long pink hair.

Answers will vary. _____

110   Classroom Connections Grade 1

Page 111

Reading Comprehension

Math
Jose has 3 erasers. His friend gives him 1 more. How many erasers does Jose have?

Jose has 4 erasers.

Language Arts
A chimpanzee was caught in a trap in 2007. She was very young. Her name was Mugu Moja. She lived in Africa. The trap was around her leg. A man took the trap off of her. Her leg was hurt. A doctor took care of her.

1. Who is the main topic of the story?
Mugu Moja

2. What type of animal is she?
chimpanzee

3. Where does she live?
Africa

Reading Comprehension

Science
Do you see a shadow in front of you? If you do, then the light is behind you. Is your shadow behind you? Then, the light is in front of you. Shadows are dark, but they are made by light.

1. Where is the light if the shadow is in front of you? behind you

2. Where is the light if the shadow is behind you? in front of you

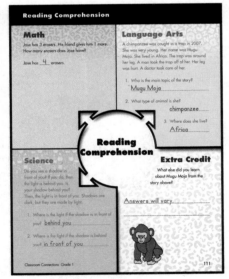

Extra Credit
What else did you learn about Mugu Moja from the story above?

Answers will vary. _____

Classroom Connections Grade 1   111

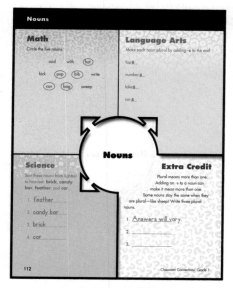

Nouns

Math

Circle the five nouns.

said with (hat)

kick (pup) (bib) write

(can) (bag) sweep

Language Arts

Make each noun plural by adding -s to the end.

top s

number s

lake s

car s

Nouns

Science

Sort these nouns from lightest to heaviest: **brick**, **candy bar**, **feather**, and **car**.

1. feather
2. candy bar
3. brick
4. car

Extra Credit

Plural means more than one. Adding an -s to a noun can make it mean more than one. Some nouns stay the same when they are plural—like sheep! Write three plural nouns.

1. Answers will vary.
2. ______
3. ______

112 Classroom Connections Grade 1

Page 112

Context Clues

Math

Mischa has 11 dolls. She gave 2 dolls to her granddaughter. How many dolls does Mischa have left?

11 - 2 = 9

Mischa has 9 dolls left.

Language Arts

To, **two**, and **too** each mean something different. Use the correct word in each sentence.

1. We went to the house.
2. There are two kids in the yard.
3. We will play at the house too.

Context Clues

Science

Fill in the blanks with the words from the word box.

beak hide roots

1. A snowshoe hare's white fur helps it to camouflage, or hide, in the snow.
2. A hummingbird's long beak helps it collect nectar from flowers.
3. Tree adapt to long periods without water by growing long roots.

Extra Credit

Circle the word that could complete both sentences.

(where) wear

1. ______ is my jacket?
2. I told Mom ______ to find the puppy.

Classroom Connections Grade 1 113

Page 113

Adjectives

Math

Write the number word that describes each group.

nine

ten

Language Arts

Write three sentences that describe the giraffe. The first sentence has been started for you.

1. The giraffe has a long neck.
2. Answers will vary.
3. ______

Adjectives

Science

Think of your sense of taste and answer the questions below.

1. What is your least favorite food?

Answers will vary.

2. Is it bitter, salty, sweet, or sour?

Extra Credit

What are three words that describe your favorite animal?

1. Answers will vary.
2. ______
3. ______

114 Classroom Connections Grade 1

Page 114

Sentences

Math

Write 14 question marks on the lines below.

? ? ? ? ? ?

? ? ? ?

? ? ? ?

Language Arts

Write a question mark at the end of each asking sentence.

1. When will Ryan get home?
2. Where is he?
3. Why is he late?

Sentences

Science

Scientists ask many questions. Fill in the blanks with letters to complete the question words.

1. h o w
2. w h y
3. wh i ch

Extra Credit

Write two questions that you would ask your favorite teacher.

1. Answers will vary.
2. ______

Classroom Connections Grade 1 115

Page 115

Verbs

Math

Write a verb to complete each sentence. Then, solve the problem. Answers will vary.

Jason ______ 5 apple pies. Then, Jason ______ 4 more apple pies.

How many pies in all?

9

Language Arts

Circle each verb.

1. Cara (calls) for her dad.
2. Eric (looks) outside.
3. Jessi (sits) in her seat.
4. Victor (plays) ball.

Verbs

Science

Circle the animals that hatch from eggs.

(birds)

(turtles)

people

dogs

Extra Credit

Think of three verbs that would tell about the way a horse moves.

1. Answers will vary.
2. ______
3. ______

116 Classroom Connections Grade 1

Page 116

Prefixes

Math

Prefix + Word = Meaning

Write the meaning of each new word.

1. re + write = write again
2. pre + game = before game
3. un + welcome = not welcome

Language Arts

Re- means **again**. Write what each word means. The first one has been done for you.

1. retest test again
2. retell tell again
3. repack pack again
4. repay pay again

Prefixes

Science

Write the foods in the correct box.

potato chips apple candy carrots lettuce cookies

Healthy	Unhealthy
potato apple carrots lettuce	chips candy cookies

Extra Credit

Name three words that have the prefix un-, which means **not**.

1. Answers will vary.
2. ______
3. ______

Classroom Connections Grade 1 117

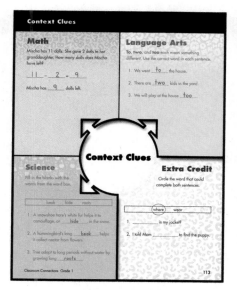

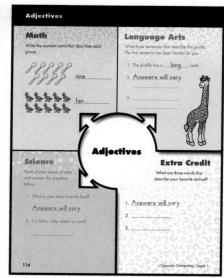

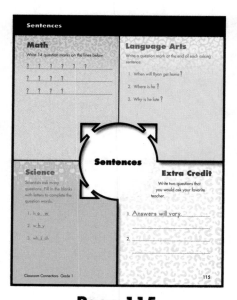

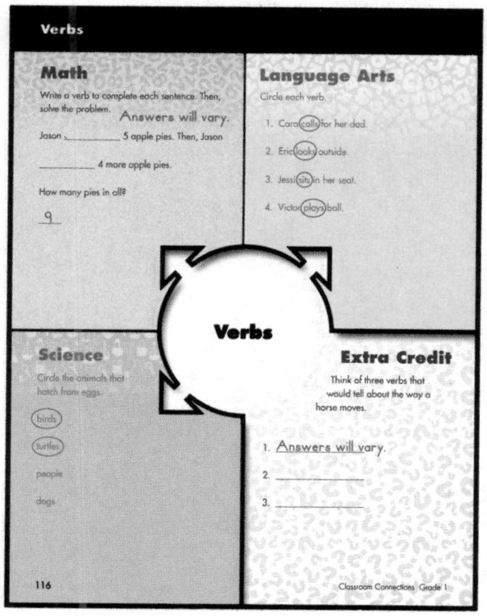

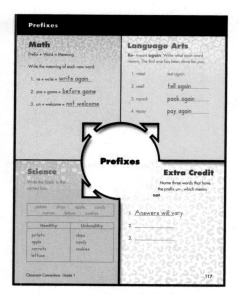

Page 117

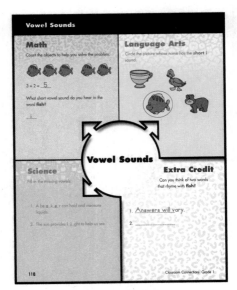

Page 118

Vowel Sounds

Math
Count the objects to help you solve the problem.

3 + 2 = 5

What short vowel sound do you hear in the word **fish**?

i

Language Arts
Circle the picture whose name has the **short i** sound.

Science
Fill in the missing vowels.

1. A be a k e r can hold and measure liquids.
2. The sun provides l i ght to help us see.

Vowel Sounds

Extra Credit
Can you think of two words that rhyme with **fish**?

1. Answers will vary.
2. _____

118   Classroom Connections Grade 1

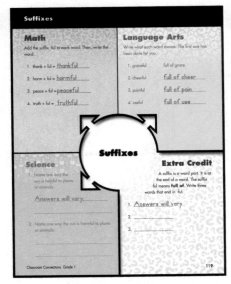

Page 119

Suffixes

Math
Add the suffix -ful to each word. Then, write the word.

1. thank + ful = thankful
2. harm + ful = harmful
3. peace + ful = peaceful
4. truth + ful = truthful

Language Arts
Write what each word means. The first one has been done for you.

1. graceful   full of grace
2. cheerful   full of cheer
3. painful   full of pain
4. useful   full of use

Science
1. Name one way the sun is helpful to plants or animals.

Answers will vary.

2. Name one way the sun is harmful to plants or animals.

Suffixes

Extra Credit
A suffix is a word part. It is at the end of a word. The suffix -ful means **full of**. Write three words that end in -ful.

1. Answers will vary.
2. _____
3. _____

Classroom Connections Grade 1   119

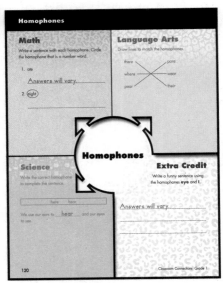

Page 120

Homophones

Math
Write a sentence with each homophone. Circle the homophone that is a number word.

1. ate
   Answers will vary.
2. (eight)

Language Arts
Draw lines to match the homophones.

there — pore
where — wear
pear — their

Science
Write the correct homophone to complete the sentence.

there   hear

We use our ears to hear and our eyes to see.

Homophones

Extra Credit
Write a funny sentence using the homophones **eye** and **I**.

Answers will vary.

120   Classroom Connections Grade 1

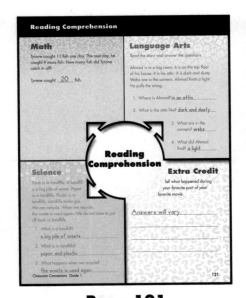

Page 121

Reading Comprehension

Math
Tyrone caught 11 fish one day. The next day, he caught 9 more fish. How many fish did Tyrone catch in all?

Tyrone caught 20 fish.

Language Arts
Read the story and answer the questions.

Ahmad is in a big room. It is on the top floor of his house. It is his attic. It is dark and dusty. Webs are in the corners. Ahmad finds a light. He pulls the string.

1. Where is Ahmad? in an attic
2. What is the attic like? dark and dusty
3. What are in the corners? webs
4. What did Ahmad find? a light

Science
Trash is in landfills. A landfill is a big pile of waste. Paper is in landfills. Plastic is in landfills. Landfills make gas. We can recycle. When we recycle, the waste is used again. We do not have to put all trash in landfills.

1. What is a landfill?
   a big pile of waste
2. What is in landfills?
   paper and plastic
3. What happens when we recycle?
   the waste is used again

Reading Comprehension

Extra Credit
Tell what happened during your favorite part of your favorite movie.

Answers will vary.

Classroom Connections Grade 1   121

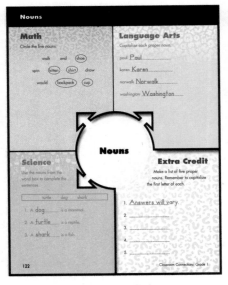

Page 122

Nouns

Math
Circle the five nouns.

walk   and   (shoe)
spin   (kitten)   (shirt)   draw
would   (backpack)   (cup)

Language Arts
Capitalize each proper noun.

paul   Paul
karen   Karen
norwalk   Norwalk
washington   Washington

Science
Use the nouns from the word box to complete the sentences.

turtle   dog   shark

1. A dog is a mammal.
2. A turtle is a reptile.
3. A shark is a fish.

Nouns

Extra Credit
Make a list of five proper nouns. Remember to capitalize the first letter of each.

1. Answers will vary.
2. _____
3. _____
4. _____
5. _____

122   Classroom Connections Grade 1

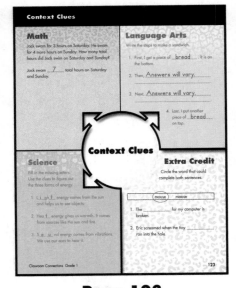

Page 123

Context Clues

Math
Jack swam for 3 hours on Saturday. He swam for 4 more hours on Sunday. How many total hours did Jack swim on Saturday and Sunday?

Jack swam 7 total hours on Saturday and Sunday.

Language Arts
Write the steps to make a sandwich.

1. First, I get a piece of bread. It is on the bottom.
2. Then, Answers will vary.
3. Next, Answers will vary.
4. Last, I put another piece of bread on top.

Science
Fill in the missing letters. Use the clues to figure out the three forms of energy.

1. L i ght energy comes from the sun and helps us to see objects.
2. Hea t energy gives us warmth. It comes from sources like the sun and fire.
3. S o u nd energy comes from vibrations. We use our ears to hear it.

Context Clues

Extra Credit
Circle the word that could complete both sentences.

(mouse)   moose

1. The _____ for my computer is broken.
2. Eric screamed when the tiny _____ ran into the hole.

Classroom Connections Grade 1   123

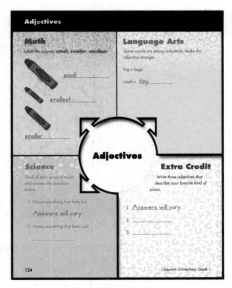

Page 124

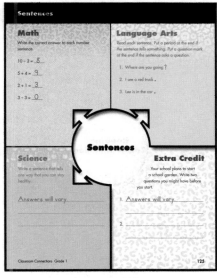

Page 125

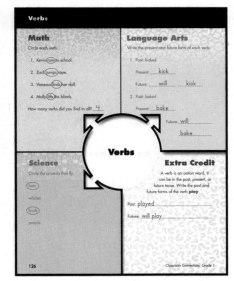

Page 126

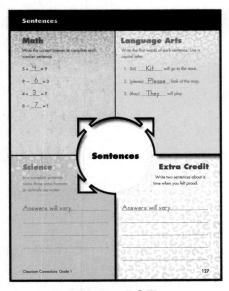

Page 127

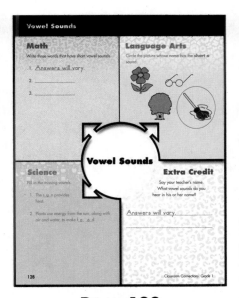

Page 128

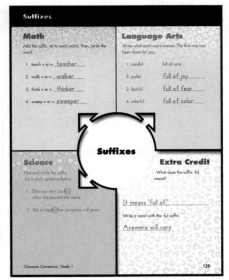

Page 129

Classroom Connections Grade 1

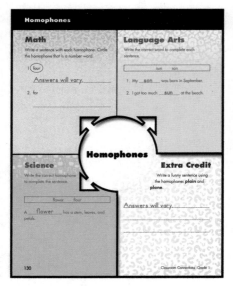

Page 130

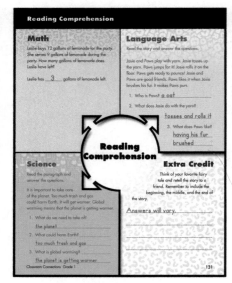

Page 131

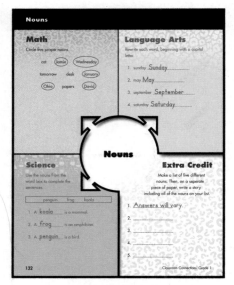

Page 132

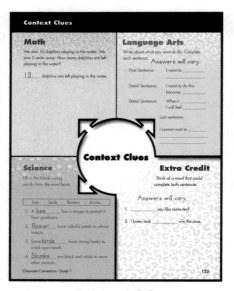

Page 133

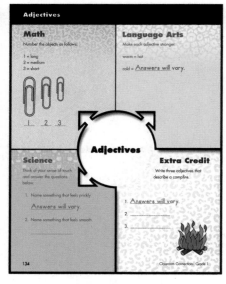

Page 134

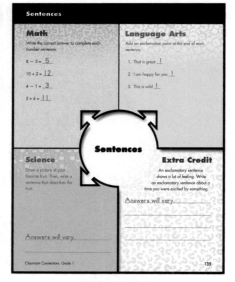

Page 135

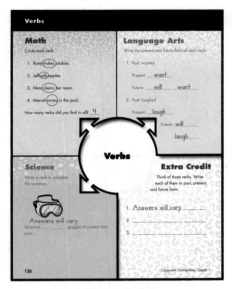

Page 136

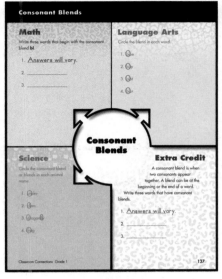

Page 137

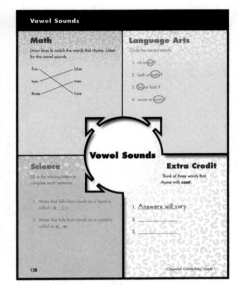

Page 138

Page 139

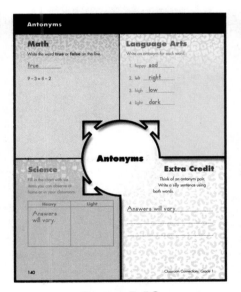

Page 140

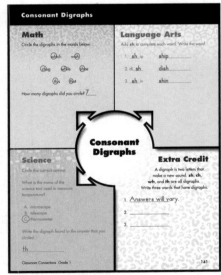

Page 141

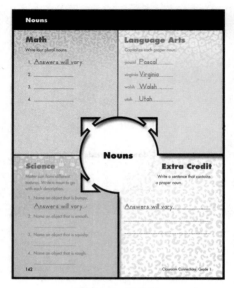

Page 142

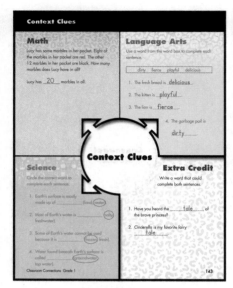

Page 143

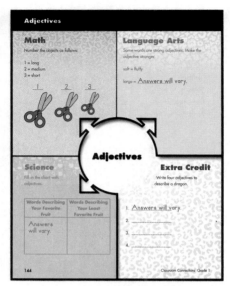

Page 144

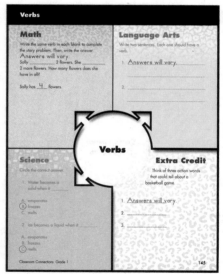

Page 145

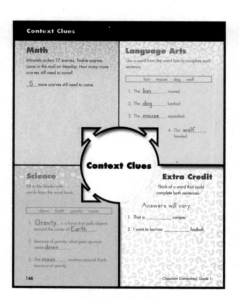

Page 146

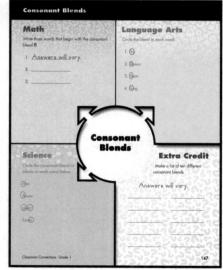

Page 147

244

Answer Key

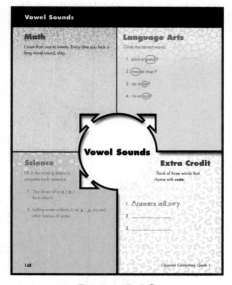

Page 148

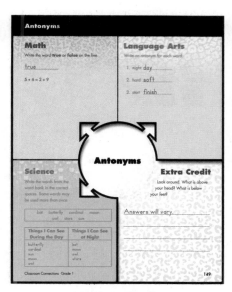

Page 149

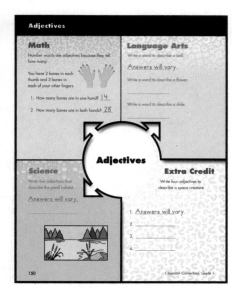

Page 150

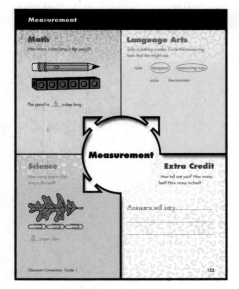

Page 153

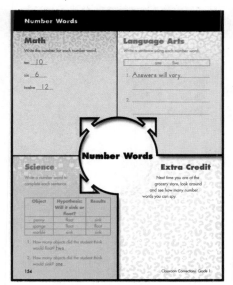

Page 154

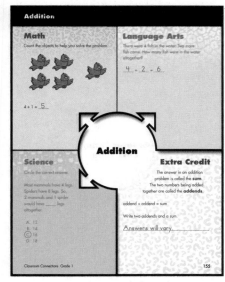

Page 155

Answer Key

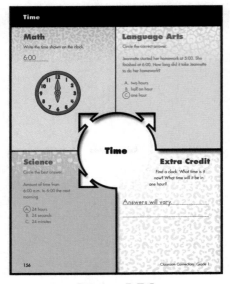

Page 156

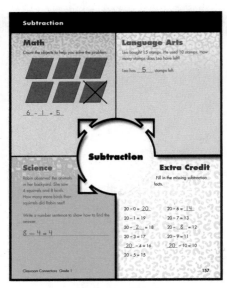

Page 157

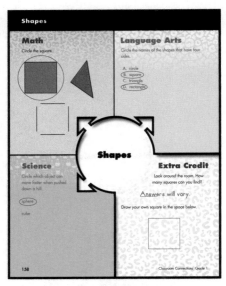

Page 158

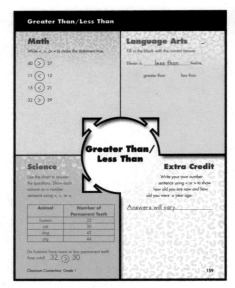

Page 159

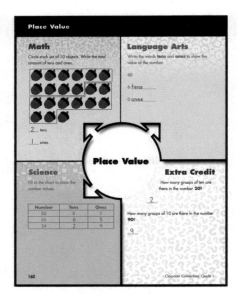

Page 160

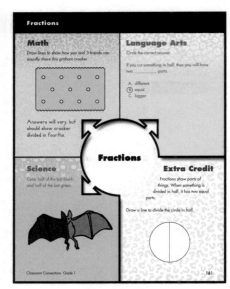

Page 161

Answer Key

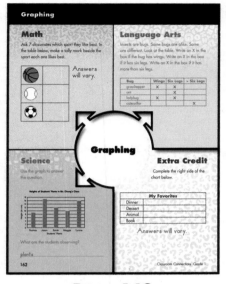

Page 162

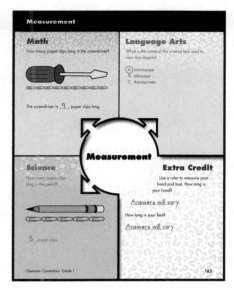

Page 163

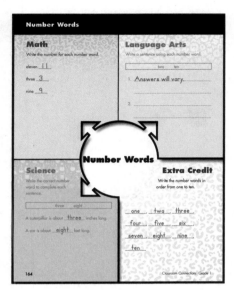

Page 164

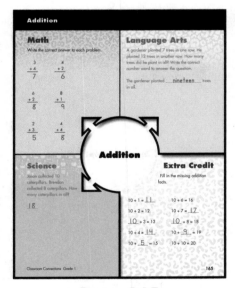

Page 165

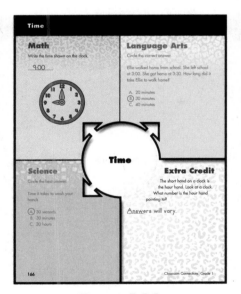

Page 166

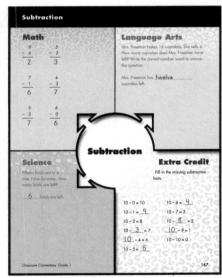

Page 167

Answer Key

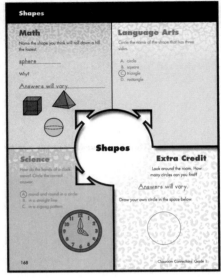

Page 168

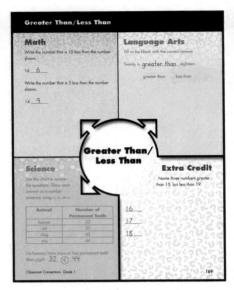

Page 169

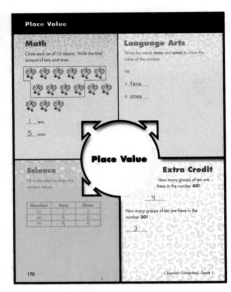

Page 170

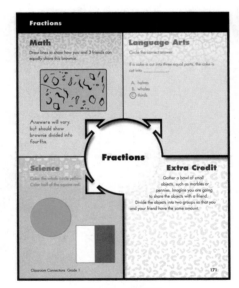

Page 171

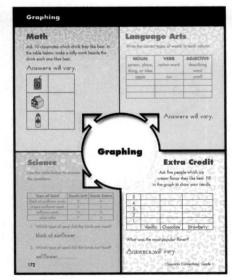

Page 172

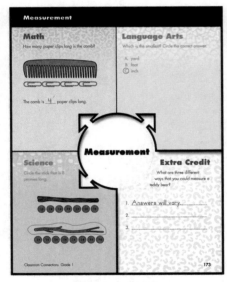

Page 173

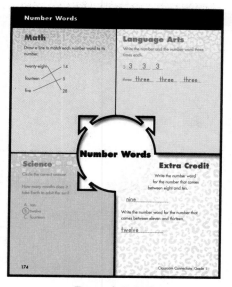

Page 174

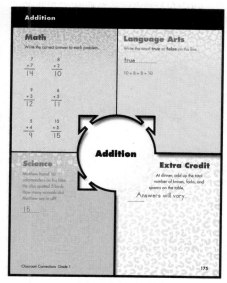

Page 175

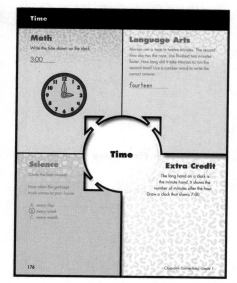

Page 176

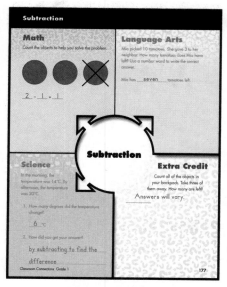

Page 177

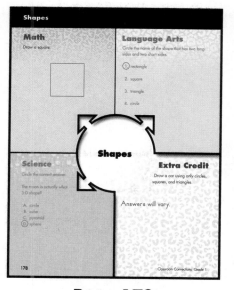

Page 178

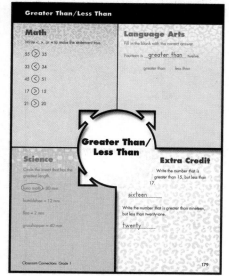

Page 179

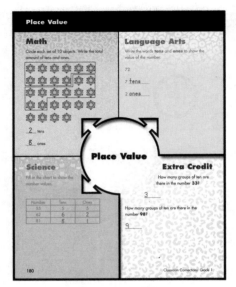

Page 180

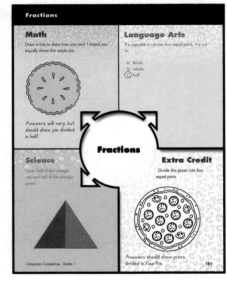

Page 181

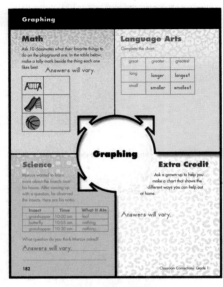

Page 182

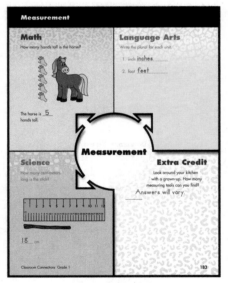

Page 183

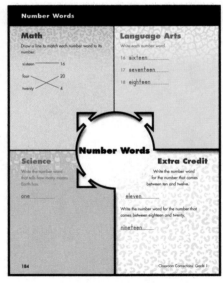

Page 184

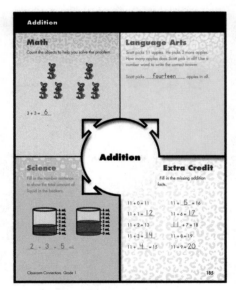

Page 185

250

Classroom Connections Grade 1

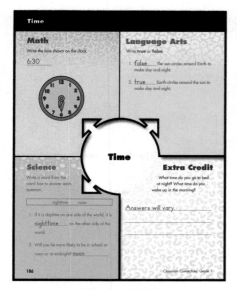

Page 186

Time

Math — Write the time shown on the clock.
6:30

Language Arts — Write true or false.
1. false — The sun circles around Earth to make day and night.
2. true — Earth circles around the sun to make day and night.

Time

Science — Write a word from the word box to answer each question.
nighttime   noon
1. If it is daytime on one side of the world, it is nighttime on the other side of the world.
2. Will you be more likely to be in school at noon or at midnight? noon

Extra Credit — What time do you go to bed at night? What time do you wake up in the morning?
Answers will vary.

186

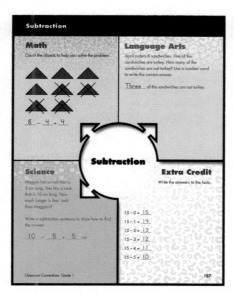

Page 187

Subtraction

Math — Count the objects to help you solve the problem.
8 - 4 = 4

Language Arts — April orders 8 sandwiches. Five of the sandwiches are not turkey. How many of the sandwiches are not turkey? Use a number word to write the correct answer.
Three of the sandwiches are not turkey.

Subtraction

Science — Maggie has a rock that is 5 cm long. Tess has a rock that is 10 cm long. How much longer is Tess' rock than Maggie's?
Write a subtraction sentence to show how to find the answer.
10 - 5 = 5 cm

Extra Credit — Write the answers to the facts.
15 - 0 = 15
15 - 1 = 14
15 - 2 = 13
15 - 3 = 12
15 - 4 = 11
15 - 5 = 10

187

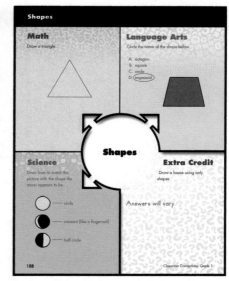

Page 188

Shapes

Math — Draw a triangle.

Language Arts — Circle the name of the shape below.
A. octagon
B. square
C. circle
D. trapezoid

Shapes

Science — Draw lines to match the picture with the shape the moon appears to be.
○ — circle
☽ — crescent (like a fingernail)
◑ — half circle

Extra Credit — Draw a house using only shapes.
Answers will vary.

188

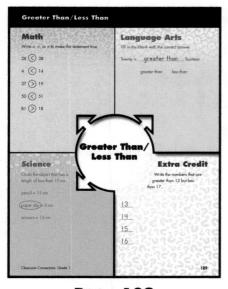

Page 189

Greater Than/Less Than

Math — Write <, >, or = to make the statement true.
28 < 38
4 < 14
37 > 19
50 < 51
81 > 18

Language Arts — Fill in the blank with the correct answer.
Twenty is greater than fourteen.
greater than   less than

Greater Than/Less Than

Science — Circle the object that has a length of less than 10 cm.
pencil = 15 cm
paper clip = 3 cm
scissors = 13 cm

Extra Credit — Write the numbers that are greater than 12 but less than 17.
13
14
15
16

189

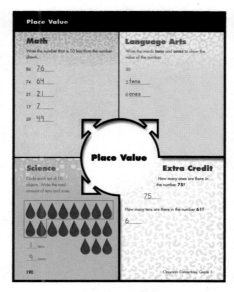

Page 190

Place Value

Math — Write the number that is 10 less than the number shown.
86 76
74 64
31 21
17 7
59 49

Language Arts — Write the words tens and ones to show the value of the number.
30
3 tens
0 ones

Place Value

Science — Circle each set of 10 objects. Write the total amount of tens and ones.
1 tens
9 ones

Extra Credit — How many ones are there in the number 75?
75
How many tens are there in the number 61?
6

190

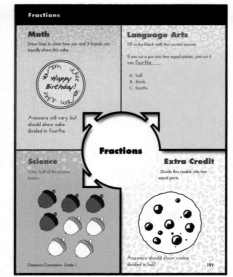

Page 191

Fractions

Math — Draw lines to show how you and 3 friends can equally share this cake.
Happy Birthday!
Answers will vary, but should show cake divided in fourths.

Language Arts — Fill in the blank with the correct answer.
If you cut a pie into four equal pieces, you cut it into fourths.
A. half
B. thirds
C. fourths

Fractions

Science — Color half of the acorns brown.

Extra Credit — Divide this cookie into two equal parts.
Answers should show cookie divided in half.

191

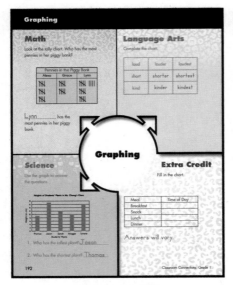

Page 192

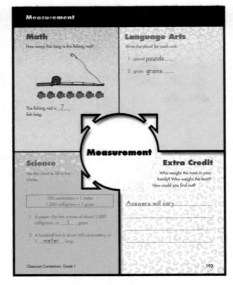

Page 193

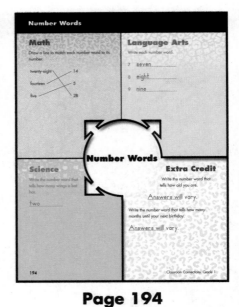

Page 194

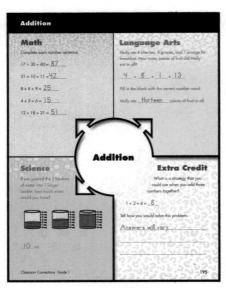

Page 195

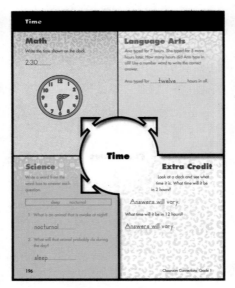

Page 196

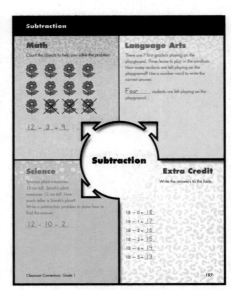

Page 197